ALL ABOUT
MOTOR
CYCLES

Written by
PEDR DAVIS
Illustrated by
BOB ARNOLD

Published by Paul Hamlyn Pty Ltd
176 South Creek Road, Dee Why West, NSW 2099
First published 1974
©Paul Hamlyn Pty Ltd 1974
Produced in Australia by the publisher
Typeset in Australia by Smith and Miles
Printed in Hong Kong
NATIONAL LIBRARY OF AUSTRALIA
CARD NUMBER AND ISBN 0 600 07194 4

Contents

THE LOCAL SCENE

MOTORCYCLES are the fastest growing part of the Australian road scene with a rate outstripping that of sports cars, sedans and other four-wheelers.

Only 5,200 new motorcycles were registered across Australia in 1963 but by 1972 sales had rocketed to 54,600 road-going machines plus an estimated 18,000 minicycles and trail bikes.

With more than 200,000 motorcycles now in use, Australia begins to rival California as a land of sunshine and cycling.

Thirty-five manufacturers offer an astonishing array of 300 different models, priced from $200 to more than $4,000.

A major surprise about the thriving industry is that no motorcycles are locally manufactured. Even though Australia has a sophisticated and profitable car industry, all motorcycles sold here are imported from Japan, Britain, Europe, America or Taiwan. In some ways this works to the advantage of the buyer, because the cream of the world's best machines is on offer with a design to suit almost every purse and purpose.

Most two-wheelers are registered for use on public roads but the numbers of unregistered off-road machines are rapidly growing. Already trail bikes, agricultural machines and minicycles account for around 25 per cent of all new motorcycles sold.

One of the world's first rotary powered two wheelers was built experimentally in Melbourne by Roger Sonnenreim in 1968 and since that time major manufacturers have adopted the Wankel rotary engine as a possible power plant of the future. Experiments with a steam powered motorcycle are now being conducted in Perth but at present all new motorcycles sold in Australia have conventional petrol engines, operating on either two-stroke or four-stroke principles. The current trend is to engines of 150 cm^3 (cubic centimetres) capacity and upwards but multicylinder machines of 500 cm^3 and greater capacity are more popular today than any time in history.

Sales in the 'Superbike' class (usually 650 cm^3 upwards) are also booming.

There is a trend to spectacular paintwork and bolt-on custom equipment which transforms the appearance of the bike, giving a distinctive identity. The use of light alloys not only improves the looks of some components but also keeps down the overall weight.

The main types of motorcycles now sold in Australia are as follows:—

MINI:

Minibikes are power-driven two wheelers with a total length not exceeding 1420 mm (56 ins). Maximum wheel diameter is 254 mm (10 ins) and maximum weight of 59 kg (130 lbs). Minicycles on the other hand are more sophisticated in design with wheels up to 405 mm (16 ins) in diameter and a maximum length of 1680 mm (66 ins).

Though some minis may be road-registered, most must not be used on public highways because they lack the equipment required for safe riding under all road conditions. The trend in the mini field is undoubtedly away from minibikes and towards powerful, faster and better sprung minicycles.

STEP THROUGH:

This is the modern equivalent of the once fashionable scooter which appeared as a city commuter after the second world war. The main difference is that today's step-through has larger wheels for greater stability. Its advantage over a normal roadster is that it is very easily mounted — a feature appreciated by the fair sex. Many girls now wear jeans when riding, so most prefer a conventional

Minicycle—with maximum overall length of 1680 mm (66 inches).

A Moped-stepthrough.

Production street-road racer.

roadster — and the step-through is losing its appeal.

ROADSTER:

This is the standard road-going motorcycle. The fuel tank is lccated between the rider's knees and the engine in the middle of the frame for even weight distribution.

The engine may vary in size from 50 cm³ capacity to 1300 cm³ or more — with a price range just as wide. Though the demand for roadsters has greatly increased in recent years, there has been a steady trend to machines with engine capacities of 125 cm³ and more. Girls find 125 cm³ and 175 cm³ machines are ideal, especially when fitted with electric starters. Young men tend to go for the 250 cm³ class.

A roadster motorcycle can be likened to the family sedan, being the volume selling, most popular and usually the most economical vehicle in its class.

SPORTS ROADSTER:

A little more expensive than a standard roadster, the sports roadster is the equivalent of the two-door coupe type car. Compared with the equivalent roadster two-wheeler, it is sportier, with a livelier engine and more comprehensive equipment.

Roadster.

SUPERBIKE:

Born with the recognition of 650 cm³ and greater capacity engines as a popular class, superbikes are the equivalent of today's high powered GT cars — the muscle cars which give effortless cruising and hair-raising acceleration. Superbikes usually have engine capacities of 650 to 1300 cm³, though engine size is less important than the overall power-to-weight ratio.

AGRICULTURAL:

Motorcycles were first used for rounding up sheep and checking boundary fences in the 1930's, but it was not until 1950 that the two-wheeler began to replace the horse for many jobs around country properties. BSA and other firms met the trend by designing special machines and from these the modern agricultural bike evolved.

Compared with a normal off-road bike, the agricultural design is geared for very slow riding. Some have a dual range gearbox, giving a choice of eight or ten forward speeds. In the lowest speeds, the rider can walk alongside the moving bike, just as a farmer can walk beside a four wheel drive utility for certain farm chores.

A large rear carrier and all-purpose tyres are necessary features.

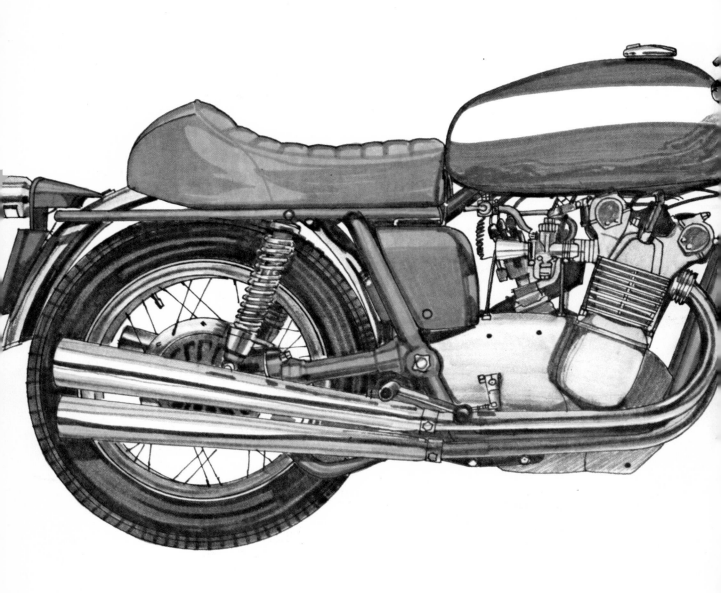

TRAIL BIKE:

A trail bike shares with an agricultural bike its lightweight design and low gearing. But it does not have a dual range gearbox and is not geared down for ultra slow progress.

Though designed primarily for use away from public roads, many are dual purpose trail bikes which can be road registered. Trail bikes are designed to handle a wide variety of terrain, from muddy slopes to rock-strewn paths. Like an agricultural design they are robust, well sprung, possessing good ground clearance and unstoppable pulling power. Engine capacities range from 90 to 500 cm³.

Nearly 20 different manufacturers offer a range of 70 trail models to serve the rapidly expanding market in Australia. Most are used as fun machines but some serve a serious purpose, such as exploration and searching for people lost in the bush.

During the past few years there have been some notable improvements in suspension systems. Whereas the typical roadster has about 89-127 mm (3.5-5 ins) of travel in its front forks, the latest trail bike design has up to 180 mm (7 ins). The suspension is better equipped to absorb severe bumps and minor collisions (with rocks or fallen trees) without throwing off the rider.

Trail bikes have greater steering head angles and front wheel trail than a roadster for maximum stability on bumpy surfaces.

Superbike.

SPORTING TRIAL:

Sporting trials have become so popular in Australia that a new class of bike is designed specifically for this purpose. Many people believe this is the sport of the future. The sporting trial bike has an impressive lock, allowing the front wheel to be turned at almost right angles to the frame. Low over-all gearing and an engine with plenty of low speed pulling power are essential features. Sporting trial bikes have tyres with treads midway between road patterns and the knobby tyres seen on moto-cross and some trail bikes.

MOTO-CROSS:

Moto-cross machines compete in events similar to rally cross for cars. They race around a short circuit specially chosen for its variety of conditions — jumps, mud, creek sand, grass. This type of sport has become so popular in Australia that Honda and other firms have now introduced moto-cross machines as production bikes. Being outright competition machines, they are not road registerable.

COMPETITION:

Apart from sporting trial and moto-cross machines, an intriguing array of other types of competition machines is built. In a later section of this book we discuss the unique world of two-wheel motor sport, so here it is sufficient to say that very specialised designs are needed to be competitive in almost any branch. There are road racing machines, grass track, speed record attempt, dirt track and even more specialist designs. A competition machine is not normally suitable for highway travel and is not registered for road use.

MOST motorcycles are conventional road-going machines but in recent years there has been an astonishing rise in sales of trail bikes, minicycles and sporting trial machines. Some can be road-registered but basically they are designed for off road use. The boom in sporting trials is a spin off from the popularity of mini and trail bikes.

Thousands of young people have graduated from recreational riding to a more competitive world where speed and skill are matched in a variety of motor sports. Moto-cross is especially popular and the growing number of devotees has led to the introduction of such specialised machines as the Honda Elsinore.

ENDURO:

Primarily built for off-road sport, enduros are equipped with small headlights and other accessories which allow them to be road registered. In the main, such machines are more at home off the road because of the type of tyres fitted, but when registered, they can be ridden to and from the terrain being explored — an obvious advantage compared with trailer-towing.

The enduro often has a sportier performance than an outright trail bike, and is more competition orientated. It is well suited to long distance trail riding on relatively good surfaces, rather than tackling tight, slow, rough trips.

The last 10 years of motorcycle sport have bred a race of tough, competitive riders from Australia and New Zealand. Like Kel Carruthers of Sydney, some have won world acclaim. This former 250cc World Champion is now Competition Director for Yamaha of America. Australian Ron Toombs campaigns with great ferocity and has won numerous Australian titles and championships.

"Iron Man" Bill Horsman won both the Australian Grand Prix and the Tourist Trophy in 1972 and also shattered the outright speed record at Bathurst. Sydney's Bryan Hindle is best remembered as the local boy who beat ten times world champion Giacomo Agostini at Oran Park Raceway. Ivan Mauger, a New Zealander, is world champion speedway rider.

Motor sport in Australia is controlled by the Auto Cycle Council of Australia, backed by more than 4 00 motorcycling clubs across the country.

It is not many years since motorcycles were mainly owned because they offered the most economical form of personal transport available. Times have changed. Today cycling enthusiasts now range from wealthy executives to office girls, from doctors to process workers. Apart from sheer convenience in congested traffic a two-wheeler is immense fun to ride. It runs on a remarkably small budget and can be parked on the proverbial dime.

Most machines are at their best on the open road. Enthusiasts believe that long distance touring is what motorcycle riding is all about. Deserted and near-deserted roads bring a tranquillity and enjoyment that a non-cyclist could never understand. Keen riders have been known to put 1600 kilometres (1000 miles) between dawn and sunset, enjoying the scenery, the rhythm of the ride and the unique relationship that exists between a good rider and a first class design.

In 1963, motorcycle sales in Australia were so low that it seemed that the very concept would soon be history. But then came a series of Japanese models, light in weight, easy to start, built with spirited performance and advanced technical design. Thus began the modern rebirth of motorcycling, which has seen sales increase ten-fold in ten years.

Though little design innovation has been done in Japan, there leading firms have been responsible for the popular acceptance of complex, multi-cylinder engines, such as overhead cam fours, modern clean styling, electric starting, big capacity two-stroke engines, five and six speed gearboxes, disc brakes, automatic clutches and in some cases automatic transmission. Most motorcycles now sold in Australia are products of advanced Japanese technology. Many of their ideas have since been adopted by manufacturers around the world

Agricultural bike.

14

Trail bike.

Moto-cross.

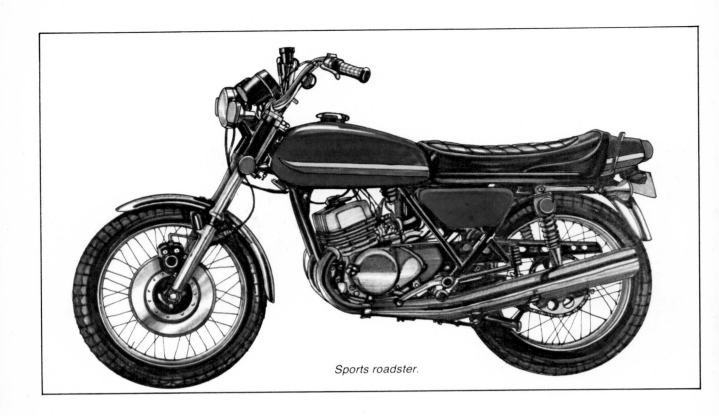

Sports roadster.

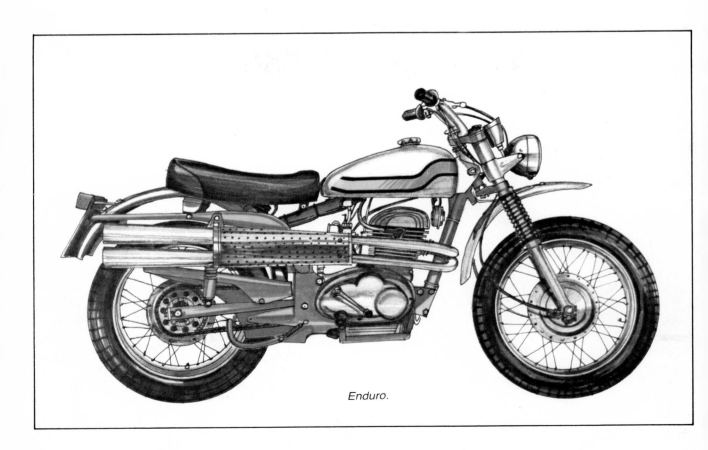

Enduro.

Sporting trial.

THE INSIDE STORY

Any two wheeled vehicle powered by a fuel burning motor can be called a motorcycle, but in practice there is a broad classification into motorcycles proper, motor scooters and mopeds — the latter being an abbreviation of "motor assisted pedal cycle". Most of the earliest designs were little more than pedal cycles aided by a small motor fitted to one wheel. Today there is still a large demand for modern motorized cycles in Europe but not in Australia.

The motorcycle, as we know it, consists of nearly one thousand parts, grouped in major components attached to a frame. The individual jobs of these components are to provide power, permit the front wheel to be steered, supply electrical energy and to give independent braking systems at the front and rear wheels. Supplementary equipment includes a saddle for riding comfort, lighting equipment, traffic turn and stop signals and

a means of starting the engine. Fuel supply, an exhaust system, transmission and suspension units are other important parts.

FRAME

The backbone of the motorcycle is its frame. Its job is to support the rider, secure all components rigidly in place and allow the front wheel to be turned at an angle for steering.

Steel tubing is commonly used because it is light, cheap and easy to bend and weld into a very strong frame.

A 'double loop' design is one in which two similar frames are joined by cross pieces, forming a cradle to support the engine, suspension struts, saddle and fuel tank. There are other ways of achieving the same result but the double loop system is widely used.

The front and rear wheels are attached to hubs which are supported by fork-like structures pivoting about the frame in conjunction with a springing system. This allows each wheel to move up and down, relative to the frame, as the cycle rides over a bumpy surface.

SUSPENSION

A springy saddle and soft tyres are not enough to absorb the road shock caused by irregular surface, especially as the speed increases. A springing system and associated parts (together comprising the suspension) are, therefore, added. The suspension provides much more than extra comfort. It helps the tyre stay firmly in contact with the ground, otherwise handling, steering and cornering ability would be greatly reduced because the wheels would bounce off the ground on bumps. Once the tyres lose contact with the ground the machine is unable to respond normally to the controls.

A typical front suspension consists of a telescopic fork in which the lower section is a tube sliding in and out of a slightly larger diameter tube known as the upper fork. The latter is fixed to the steering head, the lower section to the wheel hubs. Powerful springs inside or outside each telescopic fork help return the wheel to its normal position after a bump.

In a typical rear suspension, the fork (also called the 'swinging arm') is hinged about the frame. It pivots to allow the wheel to move up and down. A pair of spring loaded telescopic struts force the wheel to return to its normal position after a bump.

On both front and rear suspension units, the coil springs are often wound in such a way that the resistance increases progressively as the spring is compressed. For smaller bumps, the springing is soft, but it stiffens up appreciably to handle bigger bumps.

There is more to the suspension system than just springing, however. To understand why, imagine a ball suspended on the end of a length of elastic. Pull down the ball and let go and you will see the ball oscillate up and down for several seconds before becoming still. Much the same action would occur if motorcycle wheels were attached to springs purely and simply. To eliminate the bouncing tendency it is necessary to introduce a way of dampening the oscillations. There are several ways of doing this but the more common is a device known as a damper or 'shock absorber'. It is usually a telescopic design containing oil and a system of valves. When compressed, the oil is forced through a series of small holes, an action which absorbs much of the energy of the shock. The oil slowly returns as the unit regains its normal length, and the effect is to dampen the movement and greatly reduce the normal oscillation of the spring.

STEERING

A glance at any motorcycle shows that the front forks are free to pivot around a steering head which is attached rigidly to the frame. The handlebars permit the rider to move the forks to the required angle but special stops prevent the wheel being turned at too acute an angle and thereby jeopardising stability.

Wider than average handlebars allow the rider to exert more leverage. In this case the steering seems lighter, but it takes longer to turn the steering to a given angle. Short handlebars make for quicker but heavier steering, which may also be less easy to control.

A critical aspect of steering design is the angle that the forks make with the ground. This angle, known as 'rake', determines both handling and steering characteristics. The rake ensures a caster action in which the wheel always tends to return to the straight ahead position — just as the wheels on a trolley or television cabinet do. If the motorcycle forks were mounted too upright there would be insufficient caster, causing the front wheel to wobble like a hoop rolling slowly. If, on the other hand, the rake was too much, the steering would be unduly heavy because of excessive caster.

The ideal is to rake the forks just enough to give the front some 'trail'. Trail occurs when the theoretical point of contact between the tyre and the ground is some inches to the rear of where the forks would touch the ground, if they were extended by an imaginary line (see sketch). It is worth knowing that correct tyre pressures help preserve the correct trail and handling characteristics.

WHEELS AND TYRES

Though some wheels are made entirely from pressed steel, the conventional spoked rim is still very widely used, being light, strong and resilient. The wheels must run true — that is, they must be located exactly in line with the centre of the frame with no tendency to run to one side or to wobble.

Wheel and tyre sizes vary, depending on the weight and type of motorcycle involved. Tread patterns vary with the type of work they are designed to do, a knobby tyre being quite unsuitable for fast open road touring, just as a tyre built for high speed work gets nowhere in off-road muddy conditions. Tyres are a key factor in safe handling and good braking, so they should never be used after the tread depth — anywhere — has worn to 1 mm (0.04 ins) or less. Riding with a worn tyre is no wiser than riding with the brakes disconnected.

Each wheel is located on a spindle which runs in bearings held in the hub. A degree of adjustment is provided to make sure that the wheel runs true, relative to the frame and — in the case of the rear wheel — relative to chain tension.

BRAKES

Two types of brake designs are widely used — the older drum design and the more recent disc type. The basic principle is the same, however. Friction material is pressed hard against a moving metal surface, generating considerable friction which slows down the wheel. The brake heats up as a result of this friction, and is cooled by passing air.

Disc brakes have an advantage in that they cool more quickly and, under severe braking conditions, are less likely to 'fade' (that is, cease working effectively because of over-heating). As the front brake on any two-wheeler normally does about 70 per cent of the braking in an emergency stop, most high performance machines have a front disc brake and a rear drum brake.

A conventional drum brake consists of two sections. There is an outer metal drum attached to, and turning with, the wheel. Within the drum — but normally not touching it — is a pair of semi-circular shoes lined with friction material. They are anchored to the frame or suspension and do not rotate. The shoes form a complete circle, very slightly smaller in diameter than the inside of the drum; when the drum is placed over them, it can turn without touching the friction lining. As the rider applies the brake lever, however, a wedge-like cam forces the shoes apart until they rub hard against the inside of the drum.

The harder the lever is applied, the more friction is generated and the greater the stopping power. The wheel slows down rapidly and — provided that the tyre is able to maintain its grip on the road surface — the entire machine comes to a halt. Should the tyres lose their grip, however, the wheel will stop rotating and slide. Naturally, this happens more readily on a wet or loose surface.

When the brake lever is released, springs draw the brake shoes together, out of contact with the drum.

Disc brake design is different. A flat metal disc attached to the wheel takes the place of the drum. Instead of shoes there is a pair of friction pads which can be squeezed against the sides of the disc, just as caliper brakes squeeze against the wheel rim of a pedal cycle.

ENGINES

Most motorcycles are powered by a two-stroke or four-stroke reciprocating engine, so called because a piston moves up and down a cylinder. Some very interesting rotary engines are now being built for experimental and low production motor-cycles. Possibly rotary powered cycles will be mass produced in the future.

Engines are bolted to the frame, occasionally using small rubber mountings to help isolate vibration and noise. The majority are air cooled, with large metallic fins to help dissipate heat, though some are water cooled, using a small radiator to cool the water. Fuel is supplied from an overhead tank.

HOW ENGINES WORK

The decision whether to use a two-stroke or four-stroke engine is made by the manufacturer who weighs up the advantages and drawbacks before deciding which system is best suited to the machine he has in mind.

A four-stroke engine is usually heavier, more expensive and more complicated than a comparable two-stroke, but it is also more reliable in starting, gives a 'cleaner' exhaust gas and is less likely to foul the spark plugs.

Two-stroke designs have the advantage of lightness, better low speed torque and lower production cost. The main disadvantage is that lubricating oil is burned with the fuel mixture, which affects spark plug life and ease of starting.

Whether it is a two or four-stroke design, a reciprocating engine is basically a device to burn petrol and convert the resulting heat into energy. Motorcycle engines have anything from one to six cylinders — and even eight cylinder designs are mooted. Each cylinder acts in exactly the same way as the next cylinder, each being a self-contained engine. The reason for multiple cylinders (instead of one large cylinder) is that by coupling two or more to a common crankshaft, smoother power with less vibration is possible.

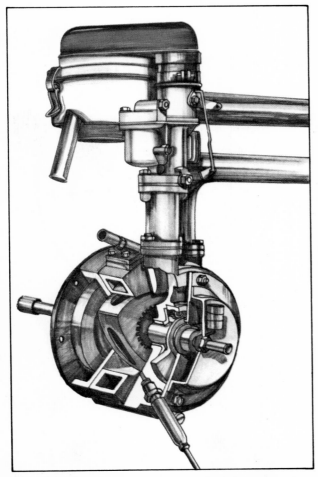

This diagrammatic layout of a Wankel engine shows the extreme compactness of the engine, especially when compared with its carburettor and air filter.

To understand how an engine works, it is necessary to consider the operation of one cylinder only, remembering that the others work in a similar way.

A cylinder is a hollow tube in which a piston moves up and down. The top of the cylinder is sealed by a cylinder head, while the piston (with built-in seals called rings) acts as a plunger to prevent gas escaping from the bottom of the cylinder. The underside of the piston is connected by a rod to a crankshaft — the latter being held in place by bearings but free to revolve as the piston goes up and down.

EXHAUST SYSTEM

If an engine was allowed to pump its burned gases straight into the atmosphere, a noise out of all proportion to the size of the engine would result. Each burst of high speed exhaust would create a sound shock wave. It is essential to add some means of baffling these shock waves and slowing them down before they reach the open air. This is done by piping the exhaust through a muffler, containing a series of baffle plates or sound absorbing fibreglass. After being suitably baffled, the exhaust gases leave the tailpipe with considerably reduced noise level.

WANKEL ROTARY

The Wankel type rotary engine operates on the same basic cycle as a four-stroke engine but instead of a piston travelling up and down a cylinder, there is a rotor spinning continuously (in one direction) inside a gas tight housing. The rotor is roughly triangular in shape and moves in an eccentric path, which is achieved by a system of internal gearing. During this motion the three corners of the rotor steadily touch the walls of the unusually shaped housing, thereby creating chambers of varying sizes. The operating cycle of intake, compression, ignition and exhaust takes place, but the main difference is that separate parts of the cycle take place simultaneously in different areas of the housing (see sketch).

FUEL SYSTEM

An engine can produce power efficiently only when its fuel is mixed with air in very carefully controlled proportions. Usually the correct figure is about 15 parts of air to one

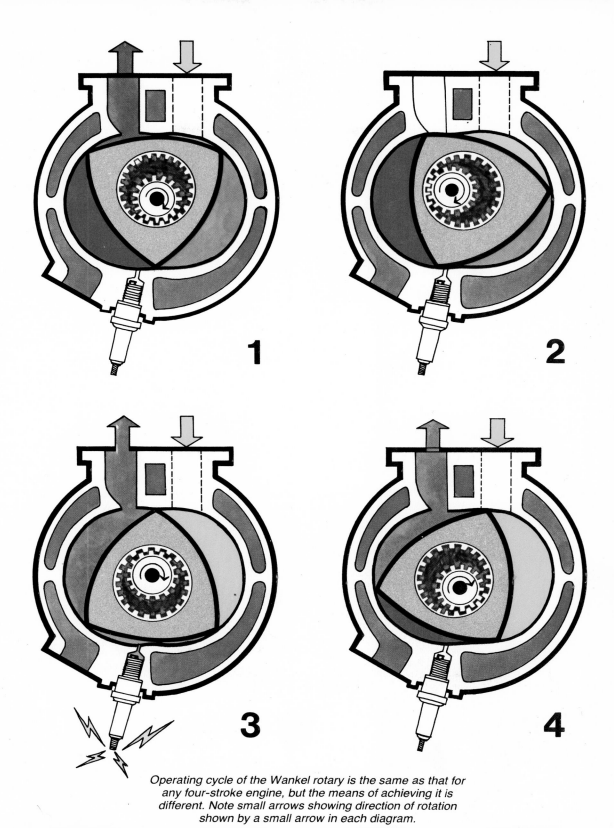

1

2

3

4

Operating cycle of the Wankel rotary is the same as that for any four-stroke engine, but the means of achieving it is different. Note small arrows showing direction of rotation shown by a small arrow in each diagram.

inlet cycle

compression ignition

expansion cycle

exhaust cycle

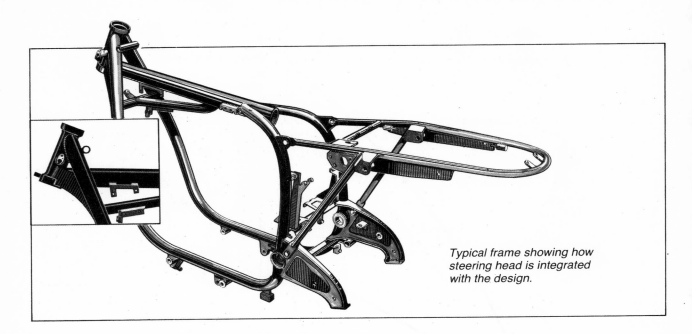

Typical frame showing how steering head is integrated with the design.

part of petrol, measured by weight. A higher proportion of petrol causes the engine to run badly, producing less power and emitting a smoky exhaust. The opposite to this 'rich' mixture is a 'lean' mixture, in which there is less than the required amount of petrol. A lean mixture burns too slowly, and may still be burning after the exhaust valve or port has opened. Damage would then result.

The job of the carburettor is to mix air and petrol in the correct proportions and make the mixture ready to enter the cylinder. This occurs when a downwards movement of the piston creates a vacuum, allowing atmospheric pressure to force the fuel mixture past the open valve or port into the cylinder.

CARBURETTOR

A carburettor works on the principle that when a restriction is placed in a pipe conveying a gas (such as air), a depression is created at the most narrow point of the restriction. (The restriction in a carburettor is known as the venturi or choke tube.) If a small jet filled with petrol is introduced into the venturi, petrol will be drawn into the passing air stream. By experimenting with jet sizes, the designer arranges the correct fuel/air mixture for the particular engine. Many carburettors have two or more jets so as to provide maximum power at varying engine speed, as well as a smooth idle.

A common way of supplying the jet with a constant supply of fuel is to build into the carburettor a 'float bowl' in which the level

of petrol is kept constant by means of a needle and valve assembly. When the needle is pulled from the valve, fuel flows in, but when the float causes the needle to press against the valve, the flow temporarily stops.

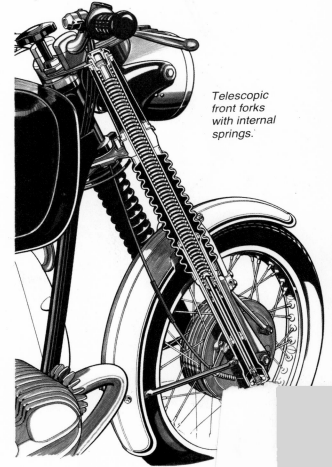

Telescopic front forks with internal springs.

22

The jet is connected to the float bowl at the same level as the top of the petrol.

IGNITION

Just before the piston reaches the top of the cylinder, on each compression stroke, the spark plug fires, causing the fuel mixture to ignite. Up to 18,000 volts are needed for a high intensity spark and this is provided by a magneto (which may be built into the flywheel) or by a coil and battery system. In addition to the high voltage electricity for the ignition, low voltage current is needed for the lights, horn, turn-signals and — if fitted — the electric starting system.

Each movement of the piston up or down the cylinder is known as a 'stroke'. The crankshaft makes one complete revolution for each two strokes made by the piston.

The length of the connecting rod is important because the piston must never quite touch the cylinder head. Instead, it leaves a gap of predetermined size when at the top of its stroke. This gap forms the combustion chamber.

Let's see what happens as a piston goes up and down.

Suppose that the piston is at the bottom of its stroke and that the cylinder is full of a mixture of petrol and air. As the piston moves up, it compresses the fuel mixture

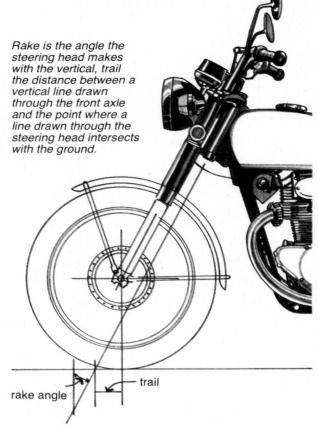

Rake is the angle the steering head makes with the vertical, trail the distance between a vertical line drawn through the front axle and the point where a line drawn through the steering head intersects with the ground.

trail

rake angle

until its volume is about one-eighth the original volume. By this time the piston is at the top of its stroke and high voltage electricity causes a spark to jump across the electrodes of a spark plug fixed into the cylinder head. The spark ignites the fuel

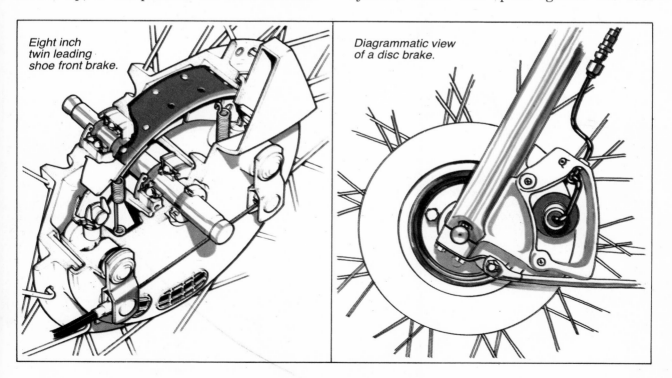

Eight inch twin leading shoe front brake.

Diagrammatic view of a disc brake.

23

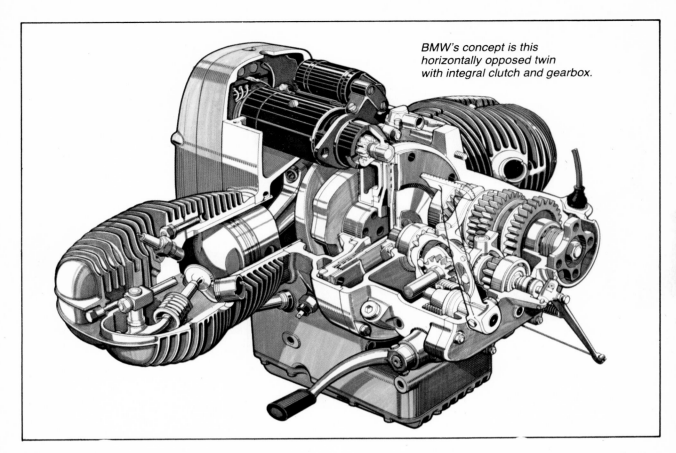

BMW's concept is this horizontally opposed twin with integral clutch and gearbox.

mixture which burns very rapidly, expanding at a tremendous rate. The resulting gas pressure drives the piston down with considerable force. The piston turns the crankshaft, to which is attached a flywheel which, in turn, is connected to the clutch.

At the bottom of its stroke the piston begins to move upwards again, this time pushing the burned fuel gases out of the cylinder. The piston next moves down the cylinder, drawing in a fresh charge of fuel mixture.

In the above cycle, the piston completes four strokes — two up and two down. In that time, the spark plug fires once, and there is one power stroke per cycle, while the crankshaft turns through two complete revolutions. This is the basis of a FOUR-STROKE design.

A TWO-STROKE is fundamentally the same, except that the above operations are combined so that the entire cycle is compressed into two strokes of the piston, with only one complete revolution of the crankshaft.

In a FOUR-STROKE engine, an inlet valve allows the fuel mixture to enter the cylinder at the correct moment; an exhaust valve permits the burned gases to leave. These valves are usually — but not always — controlled by push rods operated by a revolving eccentric shaft called a camshaft. In a TWO-STROKE engine, the movement of the piston covers and uncovers ports which control the intake of the fuel mixture and the exit of the exhaust gases. In some designs, the intake port is controlled by a rotary valve.

A variety of electric systems has been developed, some of which serve a dual purpose, providing both high and low voltage current. Others achieve the same results with two independent units. At present there is a swing towards battery-based electrical systems with coil ignition for high voltage and a generator to recharge the battery.

A spark plug is simply a component in which a central electrode is connected by wire to the high voltage supply and a second electrode (insulated from the first) is connected to the engine. A complete electrical circuit would be formed if the electrodes touched, but they are separated

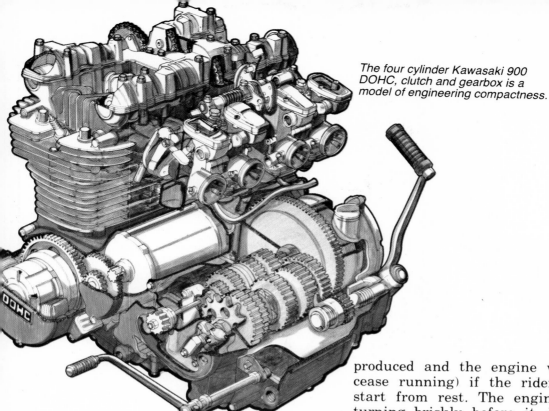

The four cylinder Kawasaki 900 DOHC, clutch and gearbox is a model of engineering compactness.

by an air gap about 0.65 mm (0.025 ins) wide. High voltage electricity jumps this gap at precisely the right time to ignite the compressed fuel mixture just when the piston is about to move down the cylinder on its power stroke.

STARTING SYSTEM

The ignition system produces no spark when the engine is stationary, so even if there is fuel mixture in the cylinder it would not fire. It is, therefore, necessary to rotate the engine briskly to make it start. When this is done, the cylinder draws in fresh fuel mixture and the plug begins to spark. Once the engine 'fires' it runs on its own accord, provided that the throttle is opened widely enough to admit fuel mixture to the engine.

Most motorcycles have a kick lever connected by gears to the crankshaft. When the lever is kicked downwards, the engine rotates. A growing number of machines have electric starters in which powerful motors take the place of the kick lever. Both kick levers and electric starters automatically disengage once the engine fires.

POWER AND SPEED

In another chapter we discuss more fully the interesting relationship between the speed of an engine and the power it develops. At slow engine speeds, practically no power is produced and the engine would stall (ie, cease running) if the rider attempted to start from rest. The engine needs to be turning briskly before it develops worthwhile torque and power; the faster it goes, the more power it develops, until the peak operating speed is reached. At higher speeds, the output falls.

Though people usually refer to the 'power' of an engine, the most significant characteristic to the rider is the 'torque'. This is the actual pulling power that the engine is

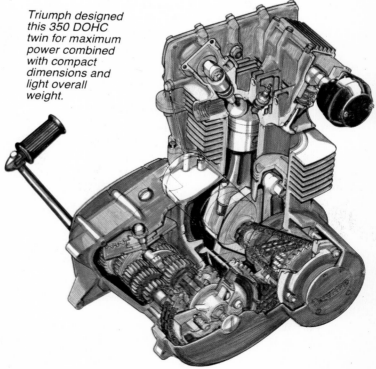

Triumph designed this 350 DOHC twin for maximum power combined with compact dimensions and light overall weight.

able to produce at a given speed. It is torque, not power, that determines whether the machine will accelerate briskly and climb hills easily.

CLUTCH

Some early motorcycles had their engine connected directly to the back wheel, so it was necessary for the bike to keep moving as long as the engine was running. Riders learned to lift the back wheel off the ground when it was necessary to keep the engine running with the bike stationary. Of course, that was not satisfactory, and designers began to introduce a clutch to allow the engine to be disconnected from the back wheel.

In some modern designs, the clutch is automatically operated, and no hand control is necessary. Such units automatically disengage at low engine speed and re-engage as the engine speed increases.

Most designs have a manually operated clutch, consisting of a series of friction discs held together by spring pressure. One side of the clutch is usually connected to the engine crankshaft, the other to the gearbox. When the springs press the discs together, the engine drives the gearbox which, in turn, drives the chain to the back wheel. But when the rider pulls in the clutch lever, a release mechanism separates the friction plates, allowing the engine to turn without

affecting the gearbox. By letting out the clutch lever smoothly, the rider is able to make a jerk-free start from rest and also disengage the gearbox when changing gears.

FINAL DRIVE

BMW and a few other designs use a geared shaft to transmit the drive from the gearbox to the back wheel. Other machines use a system of chains and sprockets.

Whatever type of final drive is used, it is necessary to 'gear down' the ratio between the speed of the engine and the speed of the back wheel. In a typical 250 cm³ street machine, the engine rotates eight times for each revolution of the back wheel in top gear. To achieve this, there is a reduction in engine speed between the crankshaft and the clutch and a further reduction between the gearbox and the back wheel. In each case, the reduction is made by having a small sprocket chain-driving a larger sprocket. For example, a sprocket with 10 teeth driving one with 20 teeth will rotate twice for every single turn of the larger sprocket.

A chain consists of a series of identical links which mate with shaped teeth on each sprocket. A connecting link turns a length of chain into an endless circle so that one sprocket can drive another as long as there is power to turn it. Correct chain tension is important, otherwise excessive wear of both

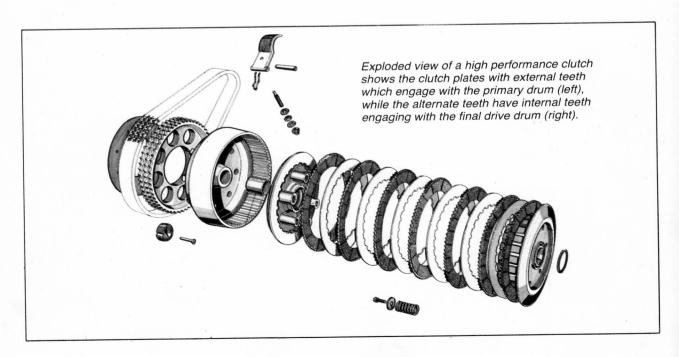

Exploded view of a high performance clutch shows the clutch plates with external teeth which engage with the primary drum (left), while the alternate teeth have internal teeth engaging with the final drive drum (right).

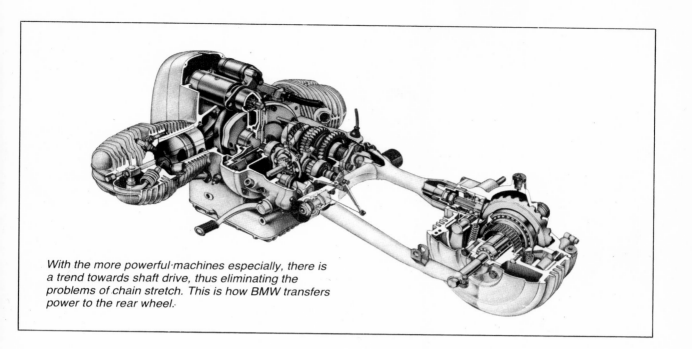

With the more powerful·machines especially, there is a trend towards shaft drive, thus eliminating the problems of chain stretch. This is how BMW transfers power to the rear wheel.·

chain and sprocket teeth takes place. A chain guard is usually provided to keep dust, fingers, clothes and dirt out of the links.

TRANSMISSION

If the perfect engine could be built, a motorcycle would need no gearbox, because the speed and output of the engine could be adjusted to suit the required road speed. In practice, an engine needs to be turning over at a speed of at least 2,500 rpm to produce worthwhile torque and power, yet the engine's maximum speed is limited to 7,500 rpm or, perhaps, a little more. This means that an engine speed range of 2,500 rpm to 7,500 rpm must be able to cope with road speeds varying from zero to, perhaps, 100 mph.

If the machine was built with one gear only, it would either have no performance whatever at low road speeds or its maximum speed would be severely limited.

To overcome this, four or more gears are provided, together with a change lever to enable the rider to select the appropriate one for the occasion. He is thus able to make sure that the engine is rotating at a comfortable speed in relation to the road speed and the amount of torque needed.

Another important consideration is that the torque can be multiplied by using a lower gear. Thus a gear giving a reduction ratio of three to one has the effect of multiplying engine torque three times. This is why far stronger acceleration is available in first gear than in the higher gears, and why a lower gear will climb a steep hill more briskly than a higher one.

The whole question of gearing and how this torque multiplication is achieved is fully discussed in the chapter on performance. Here it is enough to add that a conventional gearbox employs several sets of gears, each of which mates with other gears to provide the reduction ratio.

A more recent innovation is a type of automatic transmission, known as a torque converter. Its job is the same as that of a mechanical gearbox ie, to change the ratio between back wheel speed and engine speed. It does this automatically, using a pair of pulleys, one driving the other by means of a belt. Each pulley can enlarge or contract its effective diameter (or pitch) to provide the gear ratio required. The variable pitch pulleys automatically adjust their sizes under the influence of centrifugal force and rotating speed, providing an infinite number of gear ratios between 1 to 1 and 3 to 1.

A point worth keeping in mind is that the component containing the mechanical gears is known as a 'gearbox' but that the complete drive system, including clutch, chains and sprockets, is known as the 'transmission'.

RIGHT ROAD TO RIDING SKILL

Some interesting philosophies lie behind motorcycle ownership. Surprisingly few ride only because of the low running costs — attractive though that is. Most ride because that's their preference.

They recognise that a good rider develops an uncanny relationship with his machine. So much so, in fact, that the bike responds to his thinking process almost like a reflex action. Combined with skilful techniques and a sensible approach to road behaviour this relationship puts the rider in command of a far more responsive, interesting and mobile machine than a four wheeled automobile can ever be.

A rider enjoys wider vision than a car driver, because there is no bodywork to create blind spots and there are fewer problems with rain. He can stop more quickly, accelerate more briskly and swerve with less risk of a slide. Another advantage is that less arm and leg movement is required to operate the controls, allowing the rider to handle an emergency far more promptly than can a car driver.

Properly ridden, a motorcycle is a remarkably manoeuvrable machine, able to remain stable even if a swerve or other unusual manoeuvre becomes necessary. On the other hand, motorcycles have some basic limitations and they require a higher degree of operation skill than car driving.

Apart from exposure to wet and windy weather, the main drawback is vulnerability in an accident. As there is practically no protection, an incident that would be little more than a skirmish in a car could have painful results on a motorcycle.

Statistics show that the more experienced a rider is, the less the chance of an accident. It therefore makes good sense for young riders to start with relatively lower powered machines, graduating to bigger bikes only after several years' experience.

As discussed elsewhere, if a rider comes off his machine, the only protection comes from the helmet, shoes and riding gear he wears. Not only is it vital to wear strong protective gear at all times, but the clothing should be brightly coloured, to make the rider more visible in traffic. Though using a headlight in daylight riding is a controversial safety idea for riders, it seems to have much in its favour and is a measure well worth considering.

The most important safety measure without question is to learn proper riding techniques and to practise them at all times. Expert studies reveal that 90 per cent of road accidents are the result of human error — and there is no more certain remedy than riding correctly and sensibly.

Judgment is, perhaps, the most important of all riding skills. A person should continuously adjust his road speed to suit changing circumstances and never travel so fast as not to be able to stop within the distance of his clear vision.

Another most important attribute is anticipation. This is simply the practice of

looking well ahead, summing up movements other vehicles are likely to make — and taking evasive action before a crisis can develop. In this way, a rider stays in command of a situation and is able to avoid making hurried decisions or crash stops.

DEFENSIVE RIDING
Defensive riding is a priceless asset, for it allows safer, more enjoyable and more confident riding. Basically it is a mixture of sensible anticipation and avoiding potential trouble. Some observers call it the 'elbow room technique' because defensive riding assumes that the more free space a rider has around him, the greater the opportunity to take evasive action in an emergency.

Putting it more crudely, you never know what the fool in front, behind or at the side is likely to do. So put as much distance between him and you as possible.

You don't see expert riders squeezing between queues of traffic, swerving from lane to lane or crowding the bumper of the vehicle in front. They know better!

Colliding with another vehicle is the biggest danger that a rider faces. A recent Sydney survey shows that almost 70 per cent of motorcycle accidents within city limits involved collisions with four wheeled vehicles. The same study also showed that in 58 per cent of such accidents, the car driver was principally to blame. Unfortunately this was no consolation for the victims.

Defensive riding is based on the assumption that a rider stays away from potential trouble as best he can. He also makes himself as visible as possible, so as not to be overlooked by a driver. A surprisingly high proportion of riders does not appreciate how difficult it can be for a motorist to see a motorcycle, especially one coming from behind.

A rider finds that it pays to stay with a traffic stream, rather than fight to get ahead. He learns to read changing traffic patterns and varying road surfaces and is seldom taken by surprise. He concentrates on the road and traffic around him, ignoring distractions, worries or day dreams that might otherwise take his mind off the job in hand.

In addition to carefully watching what other road users are doing, a skilful rider makes sure that others know what he is about to do. He gives turn signals well in advance and changes direction only after double-checking with the rear vision mirror. Before over-taking, he makes sure the driver ahead knows of his presence.

A good rider meticulously obeys all road regulations, knowing well that road rules are there to protect, not bug us.

BRAKING
A keen sense of anticipation is better than a set of double disc brakes. Maximum stopping power should be reserved for those few occasions when a genuine emergency

exists. For the vast majority of stops, a rider has enough time and distance to slow down progressively and without drama — provided, of course, his sense of anticipation has been put to good use.

One problem with last-minute braking is that the vehicle behind may not be able to stop in the same distance — the reason being that a motorcycle has superior braking power to many cars. Another important point is that on slippery road surfaces, the wheels might lock up under severe braking, causing a slide.

Though motorcycles have two independent brakes, they are normally used together. In traffic situations, it is often wise to apply the rear brake momentarily before the front — thus causing the rear braking light to come on before the bike slows down appreciably.

In a panic stop situation, roughly 65 per cent of the stopping effort is made by the front brake, which is an excellent reason for ignoring that amateurish habit of using the rear brake alone. For the vast majority of road situations the brakes must be used together, with just enough pressure to provide the required stopping power.

It is important to use the front brake only when the front wheel is pointing directly ahead and to avoid using either brake on a corner because this might cause a wheel to break traction and slide. The correct technique is to slow down before reaching a bend, not afterwards.

Considerable care is necessary when braking on a slippery road surface. The right method is to squeeze on braking pressure and ease it off the moment you feel a wheel is about to lock-up and slide. When the wheel starts rolling again, squeeze on more braking pressure, but stay ready to ease off again if a lock-up re-appears. Repeat this cycle as often and as quickly as necessary to stop in the required distance. This technique allows the rider to stop in a shorter distance (with more control) than is possible with normal braking on slippery surfaces.

Being able to judge a road surface and ride at an appropriate speed is a key factor in skilful control. A rider must always remember that braking distances vary enormously with the road surface; that the limiting factor in how quickly you can stop is the amount of friction available between the tyre tread and the road surface — not how powerful the braking system is.

GEAR CHANGING
A quick way to assess the skill of a fellow rider is to watch how he changes gears. If the changes are quiet, smooth and almost imperceptible, you know he is well above average. If they are jerky, it points to inexperienced or careless riding.

All engines have a speed range in which they operate most happily. They need to be spinning fast enough to develop good torque but not so fast that they vibrate, or become noisy. Ideally, an engine should run at the minimum speed at which it spins freely without stress or lack of smoothness. To achieve this, the experienced rider changes gears as often as necessary, matching the road speed with the appropriate gear ratio that keeps the engine spinning at a happy hum.

The best operating speeds vary with different machines, so hard and fast rules cannot be offered. But when an engine begins to run roughly or fails to respond to the throttle, you know that too high a gear is engaged. A good rider does not wait for the engine to protest, however. He changes to a lower gear ahead of time, especially when crisp acceleration or strong hill climbing power will shortly be needed.

A good rider avoids slipping the clutch more than necessary, knowing that the practice creates heat and premature wear. When moving off from rest he lets the clutch lever out progressively, giving a smooth start. When changing to a higher gear, he closes the twist grip, thus slowing down engine speed to match the new ratio. But when changing down a gear, he opens the twist grip, speeding up the engine. With practice, a new rider can ensure that all gear changes are smooth and jerk-free, imposing less strain on the transmission, clutch and chains.

THROTTLE CONTROL
Ask a top line trials rider how you can improve your riding and he will almost certainly suggest that you practise throttle (accelerator) control. More than anyone else, a trials rider knows the value of feeding in precisely the right amount of power to suit the circumstances. Throttle control is just as

speed of approach when cornering. Not all these techniques can be put to use on the road because of the different conditions and because a rider cannot take 'all of the road', as he would on a race track.

Nevertheless, fundamentals remain the same. The rider does his braking and selects the right gear before reaching the corner. Having done this, he adopts the 'slow in-fast out' approach.

'Slow in' means entering the bend at a slower speed than you intend leaving it. 'Fast out' means gentle acceleration once you have reached the apex — the sharpest point of the bend.

Taking the 'right line' is the process of straightening out the bend as much as possible to give the smoothest and straightest curve through it. On a race track, you notice that riders enter a corner from the outside, cut across until they almost touch the apex, then leave on the outer side of the corner. In this way the rider follows a much straighter curve than the corner does, making faster speeds possible.

For road work, it is necessary to stay inside the lane or lanes allocated, and you cannot cut across the corner if this means obstructing other traffic. Even so, within the confines of one lane, it is possible to straighten out the curve to some extent and enjoy brisker, tidier cornering.

There is a definite limit to the maximum speed that a motorcycle can take a given corner. This has been discussed in another chapter, but here we should add that the safe maximum speed also depends on the sharpness of the bend, the tyre design and the amount of tyre grip available. Clean dry bitumen offers far more tenacious tyre adhesion than do gravel or wet surfaces. Obviously, a rider makes the necessary adjustment in his speed of approach, depending on the type of surface he is on.

A bumpy surface causes the tyre to momentarily lose contact with the ground, which reduces the overall tyre adhesion and the safe possible speed.

Knowing how fast a particular corner can be safely taken comes only from experience. The prudent rider takes all corners gently during the first few years of his riding career, building up his experience. Later when he corners more quickly he has built up a background of experience and judgment that prove invaluable.

important for road riding, of course. A rider should practise opening the twist grip no more than is essential for immediate circumstances. He needs to develop a delicate touch that sensitively adjusts to the engine's requirements. Turning the throttle wide open every time you accelerate serves no purpose — other than to waste fuel!

A good rider takes things slowly for the first few miles after a cold start, allowing the engine to warm up and circulate the lubrication oil before it is made to accelerate hard or spin at high rpm. He also appreciates the importance of opening the twist grip progressively, not snapping it open like a tap.

Most of all, the good riner knows the maximum and minimum speeds at which the engine is completely happy. He makes sure that it hums merrily in its most effective speed range.

CORNERING

Watching motor sport is an ideal way to lea the importance of balance, 'line' and

GEAR TO WEAR

To match today's motorcycles, riders choose from a variety of brightly coloured clothing that looks good, is easily visible to other road users and is as practical as the traditional gear. Not long ago standard riding rig for road use consisted of a great coat, oil skins and balaclava headgear. Today you see riders with full face helmet, leather pants, brightly coloured jacket and goat skin gloves. Many girls also wear colourful fur coverings over their helmets.

For off-road enthusiasts, there's a whole new range of gear. Specially designed boots have steel reinforcements, spreading the load across the whole foot when the rider stands on the pegs. Quilted riding suits are often too hot for vigorous off-roading, so tough weather-proofed cotton suits — material which breathes on humid days — are widely used. Moto-cross gloves have rubber backing for extra protection, in case the hand hits some shrubbery or is struck by a flying stone. Face masks, padded vests, body belts, shin guards and long sleeved skivvies are all part of the off-road scene.

Riding without protective clothing is strictly for amateurs. Not only does the right year keep the weather outside but it saves considerable skin damage in the event of a spill, whether on the highway or trail. Even taking a trip around the block in bare feet is asking for trouble; while riders who travel without a helmet have very little grey matter to protect. Australia set the lead in the compulsory wearing of helmets and major countries around the world now follow this sensible example.

The importance of colourful clothing cannot be over-stressed. Most road injuries result from a collision and fact-finding surveys show that usually the vehicle driver has failed to see the motorcyclist. The traditional dark colours worn by many riders intensify the visibility problem, which is why there is a swing to brighter clothing and helmets, plus the daytime use of headlights.

HELMETS

The compulsory use of crash helmets was inevitable as they are proven life savers. They also greatly reduce the chances of a rider or pillion passenger suffering a lifetime head or face injury.

This is the reason behind the growing number of helmets with the Ned Kelly look — the full face variety protecting the jaw, nose and cheeks as well as the head, temple and neck. Full face helmets of this type are heavier, more expensive and often less comfortable in warm weather, but they offer unequalled protection.

Another advantage of the full face type is the built-in vizor which eliminates the need for goggles and also protects spectacles against flying stones.

New full face designs are coming onto the market, aimed at eliminating the drawbacks of some earlier designs. The Italian styling house of Bertone have come up with a futuristic shape styled after the helmet and visor set-up worn during the middle ages by Knights in armour. Bertone's idea is that the vizor can be lifted up when the rider wishes to talk or clear any temporary misting problems. Fitting gear for modern knights of the road!

33

The traditional helmet shape — that of an upside down pudding bowl — is hardly worth using. It does only half a job, which is just not good enough. If you prefer not to use the full face design, the very least you owe yourself is a full jet helmet with adequate protection for jaws, ears and neck.

Whatever its shape, you cannot tell the quality of a helmet by its looks. Glossy paint and fancy decorations mean nothing when it comes to protection. What really counts is how well the helmet resists an impact and how securely it stays in place during a spill. All good helmets have a label sewn inside, listing the safety standards to which it has been tested and approved. Unless your helmet has passed top Australian, New Zealand, British or USA standards, it is obsolete and should be replaced.

To do a safe job, a helmet must fit properly and be buckled securely. It pays to shop around when buying because prices vary, as do the inside shapes and sizes of competing brands. A rider often swears by the comfort of a particular brand, while his mates find it uncomfortable. The reason is that heads and helmets come in assorted shapes and sizes, so it is worth trying on several brands until you find the most comfortable.

EYEWEAR

Unless wearing a full face helmet with built-in vizor, a rider should use a pair of goggles to keep the wind out of his eyes, as well as dust and insects. Good quality plastic goggles (some designed for ski use) give protection without misting up — a common fault where the air cannot circulate on the inside of the goggle lenses. It is important to choose a design giving a wide angle of vision, so that you can see 'out of the corners of your eyes', keeping check on traffic movements at the sides.

Never wear unprotected spectacles or sun glasses unless fitted with shatter-proof lenses. A flying stone could send slivers of ordinary glass into the eye.

JACKETS AND TROUSERS

Bitumen and concrete are hard and very abrasive, which is why the tyres are able to get a good grip. Should you take a tumble, your elbows, hands and knees are very easily skinned. Suitable clothing provides valuable protection that no rider (or passenger) can afford to be without.

Leather will always be popular with riders because it is tough, good looking and immensely durable when treated properly. Unfortunately, it is rather expensive, a little hot in summer, and may be a little less water-proof than some artificially proofed riding suits. Even so, for general purpose road riding leather is not far short of ideal. Proofed nylon and PVC suits — in a variety of bright colours — are immensely practical for road use and their bright hues make them safer than the traditional dark shades.

Fully quilted riding suits are fine for road use on cool days and girls especially go for the black 'wet look' vinyl gear. In many ways the most practical of all suits for serious riding is the waxed cotton type. Originally introduced for trials riding, because it is thoroughly waterproof, waxed cotton suits are widely used for a variety of riding conditions. They usually have plenty of pockets with weatherproof flaps, plus added protection over the zippered openings. Some cotton suits are lined, with inside pockets; some are a two-piece design, the pants having an elasticised waist, with openings to the pockets in clothes underneath. Usually the seats and knees have double reinforcements, with wide gussets at the bottom to slip over riding boots. Prices range up to $75, not cheap, of course, but the cost should be spread over a life-time of riding.

Waxed cotton suits have one disadvantage for daily commuting. The oil-like proofing tends to come off on the fingers (and clothes), especially when the suit is new. On the other hand, the material breathes well in hot weather and is more suitable for vigorous off-roading.

On the subject of off-roading, special moto-cross breeches, made from leather and fully lined for warmth are priced around $60.

GLOVES

Gloves protect the hands against scratches from tree branches, burns from the engine or exhaust pipes and from flying stones. Many are designed to absorb perspiration, reducing that clammy feeling. On cool days they keep the fingers warm and supple.

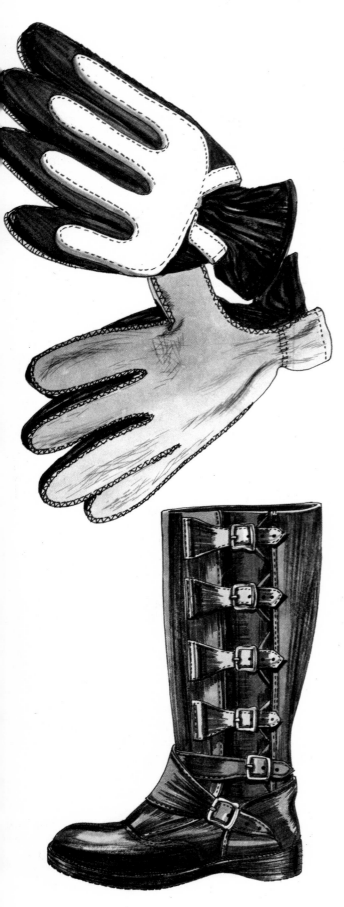

Riders who do not like wearing gloves should try fingerless mittens which absorb moisture but leave the fingers free to manipulate the controls. Some leather gloves have the unfortunate habit of leaving near indelible stains on the hands, a point worth checking when making your choice.

A popular type of glove is made from goat skin, with rot-proof terylene stitching. Lightweight, plastic material on the back is able to absorb the impact of flying stones or knocks from light tree branches.

FOOTWEAR

Feet and ankles are vulnerable, especially when riding close to the undergrowth on trails. As you do not want your toes to tangle with passing shrubbery, adequate protection is essential.

Only rank amateurs wear thongs or ride with bare feet. Whether on the road or trail, experienced riders use boots that at least cover the ankles. Most top quality boots are calf-length with strong buckles at the side to ensure strong support. Full length boots are mandatory for most competitive events.

Like riding suits, boots tend to be specialised, depending on their use. Up to $60 can be paid for a really good pair of moto-cross boots, with strong ankle support and special soles and heels to spread the load when standing on the foot pegs. Warmth is important, of course, and for long distance touring fleecy lined boots are hard to beat. High grade leather is still the most popular material for quality boots, though various man-made substitutes are gaining a sizeable share of the market.

POWER, PACE AND PERFORMANCE

Ever considered the difference between a 'quick' and a 'fast' bike!

The first is capable of a good all-round performance, whereas the second is merely a machine with a high top speed.

A bike is said to be 'quick' when capable of making rapid progress between two points. To do so needs brisk acceleration, tenacious handling qualities, powerful brakes as well as a high cruising speed.

A powerful engine is not enough by itself. Unless matched by a first-class suspension system and suitable gearing for the type of work involved, the machine cannot be a good all round performer.

Even the engine must suit the purpose. A racing design would be quite hopeless in city traffic, for example, while a touring engine with outstanding top gear flexibility might be completely outclassed on a racing circuit.

It is not possible to design into one engine the best of all desirable characteristics, such as maximum power, smoothness, flexibility, quietness, easy starting, good fuel economy and fuss-free high speed running. So a designer compromises. He accentuates those characteristics that he wants for a particular purpose, knowing that other desirable characteristics must suffer. If he wants an engine that pulls crisply from a low speed in top gear, then maximum power, to some extent, must be sacrificed. Similarly, a designer seeking maximum power cannot expect good fuel economy and smooth low speed performance as well.

All road-going machines represent a designer's interpretation of the most acceptable compromises for the job in hand — which is why there can be big differences in temperament, feel and performance between rival machines. Basically, though, all designers encounter the same problems and the same design limitations.

At slow speeds, for example, an engine develops practically no power and would stall if the rider tried to move off with the throttle almost closed. But as engine speed increases, power builds up rapidly, until the peak power output is reached at a given speed. For example, a typical 350 cm³ twin develops 45 horsepower (35 kw) at 8,000 rpm. It can be revved to higher speeds, but the power output would fall above 8,000 rpm.

As mentioned earlier, the most important characteristic of an engine is its torque output. Torque is the twisting force exerted by the engine — the force that causes the crankshaft to drive the transmission.

Torque output is negligible at low engine speeds, increasing as the engine speeds up. Eventually a peak output is reached and at higher speeds still the torque output falls. In the case of the typical 350 cm³ twin, maximum torque is 39 nm (or 29 ft/lbs) at 7500 rpm.

Torque is important because it makes the difference between brisk and tardy acceleration. It also determines the horsepower as the power that an engine develops at a given speed is directly proportional to the torque.

An interesting phenomenon is that torque can be multiplied to provide brisker acceleration or better hill climbing when needed. In fact, every time a rider changes to a lower gear torque output is multiplied.

To understand how this is possible, consider a crowbar with a pivot near one end. Using this crowbar, it is possible to lift a very heavy object — such as a large rock — which you could not normally move with your bare hands. The reason is that a crowbar is a device to multiply the lifting effort. The multiplication is proportional to the distance between the crowbar's lower end and the pivot compared with the distance from the pivot to the point where your hands exert force. Suppose that this ratio was 8 to 1. This means that the crowbar could multiply lifting effort eight times. If you were to lift the rock 6 cm, it would then be necessary to move the long end of the crowbar a distance of 6 cm multiplied by eight — or 48 cm.

By moving the pivot point closer to the centre of the crowbar you can reduce the multiplication factor and with it the distance that the long end has to be moved. Put the pivot in the centre of the crowbar and there would be no leverage advantage. The exact effort you applied at one end of the bar would be transmitted to the other end, without multiplication.

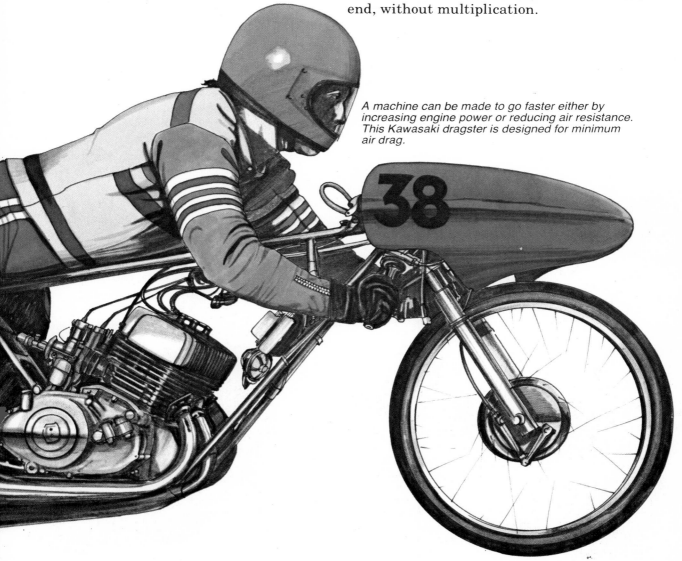

A machine can be made to go faster either by increasing engine power or reducing air resistance. This Kawasaki dragster is designed for minimum air drag.

The same basic principle applies with the gears of a motorcycle.

When a small gear has its teeth meshed with a larger gear, the large gear turns at a slower speed than the small gear. If, for example, the large gear had four times as many teeth as the small gear, it would turn at one-quarter the speed. At the same time it would multiply the torque four times.

Suppose that a motorcycle gearbox has four gear ratios. Low gear has a multiplication factor of four; second gear a multiplication factor of three; third gear a factor of two; top a factor of one. In this case, top gear would be called 'direct' and can be likened to having the pivot in the centre of a crowbar. There would be no change in the torque output.

Now let's assume that an engine is turning over at a speed of 5000 rpm. Let's also assume that this gives a road speed of 96 kmh (60 mph) in top gear. If the rider was to change to third gear, the equivalent

road speed would be 48 kmh (30 mph) but engine torque would double. A change to second gear would give a road speed to 32 kmh (20 mph) with three times normal engine torque. In bottom gear, road speed would be 24 kmh (15 mph) with four times as much torque.

In practice, motorcycle gear ratios are much closer than the above illustrations, which are given to simplify the explanation. But it is easy to see why first gear has the briskest acceleration and limited maximum speed. Second gear has less torque but a higher speed. Third gear has even less torque and a faster road speed again. Top gear offers the least torque of all but the highest road speed. In addition, top gear gives the best fuel economy and the lowest engine noise, because for any given road speed, the engine is turning over at a slower speed than it would in a lower gear.

Top gear is said to be 'flexible' when the engine is able to pull smoothly with reasonably good acceleration at a relatively slow speed. But it is usual to change to a lower gear, not only to have ample acceleration available when required, but to allow the engine to spin more briskly. An engine is never happy (nor operating efficiently) when allowed to labour at low rpm.

Apart from the use of the gearbox, it is also necessary to gear down the speed of the back wheel relative to the engine. In a typical 350 cm³ machine the engine turns through seven revolutions in top gear for a single turn of the back wheel. This reduction is achieved by using different size sprockets between the engine and the back wheel.

Many factors are taken into account when deciding on the overall gear ratio, but the aim is to have fairly high gearing to allow fast cruising speeds with minimum fuel consumption. As a rule of thumb it is desirable for the bike's maximum speed to coincide with the engine's rpm at which maximum power is developed. If this happens to be 8000 rpm and a speed 160 kmh (100 mph) was sought, the designer would calculate the exact gearing necessary to allow the machine to be travelling at 160 kmh (100 mph) in top gear when the engine was doing 8000 rpm.

The bike would, however, only achieve the required 160 kmh (100 mph) if its engine

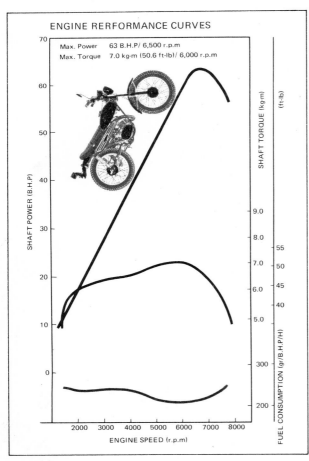

A motorcycle engine has many characteristics, not the least of which is that power output and torque increase with engine speed until a maximum is reached.

could develop enough power to overcome the mechanical and wind resistance encountered at that speed. If it did not develop enough power, the designer would have to settle for a lower top speed and gear the bike accordingly.

Wind resistance is the big factor in limiting maximum speed. The faster anything travels, the greater the air drag. In mathematical terms, air drag is said to increase with the square of the speed. That is, if you double the speed, you meet with four times the wind resistance. Frictional resistances within the transmission and wheel bearings also increase with speed. A typical cycle might, therefore, need 6 kw (8 hp) to achieve 96 kmh (60 mph), 18 kw (24 hp) for 162 kmh (90 mph) and 37 kw (50 hp) for 192 kmh (120 mph). The actual power depends on the frontal area of the combined cycle and rider, which is why crouching over the handlebars raises maximum speed a little. At higher speed it takes a big increase in power to gain a small increase in speed. Correct gearing is most important as it is essential that the engine be developing its maximum power at the intended top speed.

One way of raising top speed without an increase in power is to reduce the air drag. This can be done by the use of aerodynamic fairing — or streamlining as it is sometimes called.

So much for maximu speed. But, as we discussed earlier, a cycle is only 'quick' if it has good road manners, allowing rapid cornering in safety.

Handling is the least tangible form of performance to assess. It cannot be readily measured, like acceleration, fuel consumption or maximum speed, yet good handling is important in the interests of fast travel as well as the safety and comfort of the rider.

When a cycle goes around a corner, a variety of forces come into action. One is centrifugal. This is the same force that keeps a yo-yo tugging on the end of the string when you whirl it around your head. The faster a cycle goes around a corner, the greater the centrifugal force, creating a tendency to run off the corner instead of following the line that the rider wishes to take.

When taking a bend at a steady speed, a rider and his machine automatically lean inwards at an angle such that the

C of G

centrigugal force

resultant force passing through tyre contact plane

gravitational force

This diagram shows how centrifugal force and the weight of a machine combine to form a larger force that passes through the point of contact with the road.

centrifugal force acting outwards through the centre of gravity is exactly balanced by the tendency of the bike and rider to fall inwards. A condition of equilibrium is reached, but a limiting factor is always how much grip exists between the tyre (at the point of contact) and the road surface. Only if centrifugal force becomes greater than this grip will the cycle slide outwards. The grip, however, varies considerably, with different types of road surface, especially when wet or muddy. Tyre patterns and pressures also play an important part.

To ensure sound safe handling, the basic design of the machine must be correct. The frame should be stiff enough to hold all components, especially the wheels, in perfect alignment. The suspension must be capable of keeping the tyres firmly in contact with the ground, even over bumps. The centre of gravity should be as low as practical.

Only when the motorcycle has been correctly designed from tyres to steering head can it be 'quick' as well as 'fast'.

SPORT, SPEEDWAY AND SPEED RECORDS

Ever since motorcycles first appeared there have been arguments about the merits of rival designs. Speed and reliability have long been the great deciders, so it is little wonder that motorcycle racing dates back to 1897 when some machines were timed at the then preposterous speed of 43 kmh (27 mph). For five furious years, rival manufacturers fought it out, often winning races by the width of a tyre tread.

In 1903 Frenchman Maurice Fournier built a 2344 cm³ twin cylinder racing machine developing 22 horsepower. Newspapers of the day described it as a 'speed monstrosity' and their worst fears were confirmed when Fournier shattered all existing records with a speed of 128 kmh (80 mph). Despite statements by eminent scientists that the human constitution could not survive such speeds, Fournier proved none the worse for his ordeal.

Progress in the search for higher speeds was much slower after this milestone. It was not until 1920 that a cycle rider reached 162 kmh (100 mph). This particular record helped put Australia on the motorcycling map, because it was achieved in South Australia by Arch Smith. A less spectacular world record was established 'down under' in 1932 when J. Illich achieved a petrol consumption of 370.4 miles per gallon (0.76 litres per 100 km) with a 247 cm³ Ariel.

Organised motorcylce racing dates back at least to 1903 when Genty on a Griffon won Europe's first speed trial, averaging 97 kmh (61.5 mph).

In that year, the Pioneer Motor Cycle Club of NSW was formed, quickly followed by similar organisations in other States. During 1905 and 1906 motorcycles took part in the Melbourne-Sydney car races organised by Dunlop.

Motorcycle sport was here to stay!

In most ways, Australian riders were content to follow overseas activities, though they earned a well deserved reputation for

Two-wheeling is very much part of the action with three-wheeled outfits. Canberra rider John Grant tries balancing his Honda 750 on two wheels while his passenger does his best to hang on.

improvisation, especially when it came to fabricating home-made racing machines. But Australians pioneered one form of sport which is now the most successful motorcycle spectacle around the world in speedway riding.

In 1922 stripped-down road cycles were raced on loose surface track as a special attraction during a NSW agricultural show. The idea proved immensely popular and was quickly adopted overseas. Almost by accident Australia gave birth to dirt track racing, the forerunner of the modern more sophisticated speedway racing.

During the past few years motorcycle sport has changed in character enormously. Australian riders have progressed from a band of dedicated amateurs with improvised machines to world class riders using expensive imported equipment. The first Australian to compete successfully as an international was Victorian Ken Kavanagh, winner of the 1956 350 cm³ world championship. Five years later another Aussie, Tom Phillips, won the 125 cm³ world title. Since 1969 Kel Carruthers of Sydney has kept the Australian flag flying at the international arena. Australian Jack Findlay is also very successful overseas at the present time. In the 1973 Isle of Man TT, he became the first Australian to win the much coveted 500 cm³ Senior TT.

JOINING IN COMPETITION

An introduction to competitive motorcycle sport is possible by joining one of the 400-odd recognised motorcycle clubs scattered throughout the country. The clubs are affiliated, through the State Local Controlling Bodies, with the Auto Cycle Council of Australia (ACCA), the controlling body of all forms of motorcycle sport in Australia. International recognition is gained through the ACCA.

Competitors need a special licence which, under present legislation, means a minimum age of 17 years. More than one quarter of the 40,000 club members in Australia hold competition licences — evidence of the exceptional popularity of motorcycle sport.

Most clubs organise a wide variety of competitive events, including gymkhanas, treasure hunts, sporting road trials, scrambles, moto-cross and, in some cases, road racing. Competitors are usually graded (A, B and C classes) depending on skill and experience, and this allows rank amateurs to enter many club events without being out of their depth.

Most riders compete purely for pleasure. It is almost impossible to make a living as a full-time racing rider in Australia. Even top contenders are happy to cover expenses only with prize money.

ROAD RACING
Contrary to its name, road racing today is not done on public highways, except when specially closed off by the police as at the meeting at Bathurst Mount Panorama circuit. Road racing did, however, begin its life on public roads.

Road racing is competition in its purest form — man and machine against man and machine, skill against skill, courage against courage. The fastest combination wins and close racing can be the most exciting and spectacular combat of all. To ensure even competition, machines are divided into three categories — production, modified production and racing machines. The production cycles have to be completely stock-standard, so victory in a production race bestows glory on the manufacturer as well as the rider.

Competing machines are also classified by engine capacity — Ultra-lightweight (up to 125 cm³); Lightweight (126-250 cm³); Junior (251 to 350 cm³); Senior (351 to 500 cm³) and Unlimited (normally up to 1300 cm³).

Some races consist of a fixed number of laps, the first rider to complete them being the winner. Other events, such as the Castrol 6 Hour, are won by the rider who travels the longest distance in a given time. The Australian Grand Prix — a premier series — is contested over six rounds, one event in each State. Class winners are those who amass the most points over any four meetings.

Road racing draws tremendous crowds. Oran Park in NSW has attracted as many as 1000 competitiors and 20,000 spectators to a single meeting. The Bathurst Easter races attract nearly as many spectators despite its distance from a capital city. Most race day field events cover production and racing cycles, with side-car and perhaps vintage events for variety.

Side-cars (or 'chairs') introduce an ex-citing new element to racing because the passenger uses this weight to assist the rider take all corners at maximum speed. Side-cars are propelled by racing machines, not production designs, and are divided into junior (up to 650 cm³) and senior (up to 1300 cm³) classes. Side-car events are popular because they provide spectators with spectacular thrills as well as keen, tightly contested racing.

At the time of writing, the fastest racing bikes in Australia are a Suzuki TR750 and a works Kawasaki. Specially built for the fast Daytona series in the USA, the Suzuki has a speed potential of 304 kmh (190 mph) and has been timed at 278 kmh (174 mph).

OFF-ROAD-COMPETITIONS
Less glamorous than road racing, off-road competitions are particularly exciting for competitors and spectators. Off-road sport is becoming so popular that manufacturers now design a selection of models specially engineered for off-road competition. It is difficult to make clear distinctions between such events as 'trials', 'sporting trials', 'scrambles', 'enduros', 'moto-cross' and 'cross country racing' because there are shades of meanings, varying from State to State and even club to club. Some events are virtually an amalgamation of two or more other events.

SCRAMBLES AND MOTO-CROSS
Though the worlds 'scramble' and 'moto-cross' are often interchanged, there is a distinction. A scramble is over a given number of laps and each event is a complete race. In moto-cross, riders usually race for a given time and a day's racing often has two events per day per class, points being scored in each to decide the overall winner and place getters for the day.

In most cases a scramble course includes a variety of man-made obstacles, whereas moto-cross is normally held on natural terrain. Scramble circuits tend to be shorter than moto-cross, tighter and, perhaps, rougher. In both cases competitors race against each other over a tricky course that takes considerable skill to negotiate. Top riders, such as Australian champion Dave Basham, are equally at home in scramble and moto-cross events.

There is no mistaking the riding style of world champion Giacomo Agostini during his Australian tour.

Scrambling began in Britain in 1927 when a group of riders organised a race over the wildest ground they could find. It was a novel idea at the time and one of the organisers unwittingly coined the name when he predicted that the race would develop into a 'rare old scramble'. This it did! Half the 80 starters dropped out before the race was over, but everyone loved it and a new sport was born. Scrambling spread to Europe, Australia, New Zealand and Japan and is now second only to road racing in popularity.

Almost every Australian country town has a suitable track, with the number of enthusiasts growing by the month. Some championship events, such as those held at Mulbring, NSW, and Basham Park, South Australia, attract as many as 400 entries and 10,000 spectators.

TRIALS
Trials are events of skill but not of speed. It does not matter how slowly a rider travels. The object is to complete a difficult course without falling off or putting a foot on the ground.

A trial is held on the roughest, toughest course the organisers can find. It takes very exceptional skill to tackle some sections without 'dabbing' a foot on the ground. Each dab means the penalty of a point, the winner being the rider incurring the least number of points.

Some years ago champion trials rider Sammy Miller visited Australia and gave a series of trial schools which enormously raised the standard and enthusiasm for this branch of motor sport.

A trial can be staged in a very confined area, if necessary, and there is minimal risk of anyone being hurt. Bultaco, Montesa, Kawasaki, Honda, Yamaha and many others produce models specially designed for trial riding.

ROAD AND RELIABILITY TRIALS
Often (but not always) held on public roads, these trials are strictly competitive events but not races. They are a test of a rider's ability to navigate and maintain a set average speed over unfamiliar (and often challenging) terrain, embracing a wide range of conditions.

A road trial is usually divided into stages, each of which must be completed at a set average speed. Points are lost for arriving late or departing from a set course. A typical route might cover 96 km (60 miles) on a Saturday afternoon or 256 km (160 miles) for a full day's riding on Sunday. There may be some fairly rapid cross-country riding, narrow forest trails, bush tracks and 'transport' sections on the open road.

As in other sports, riders are graded by skill and experience, with different average speeds expected from each grade. Honda, Yamaha, Suzuki and Kawasaki all do well in road trials.

Top: *Victorian rider Mike Tankard falls almost under the wheels of Wollongong rider Terry Gunter (No. 117) Guido Simionato (CZ No 18). takes avoiding action behind.*

Bottom: *Cycle car racing in moto-cross introduces a new and exciting element to an already adventurous sport.*

ENDURO RACING

Especially popular in Victoria, West Australia and Queensland, enduro races are hell-for-leather dashes across private property. Racing on public roads is illegal in these States and enduro events are not held on land to which the public has free access.

The length and type of event varies considerably. The annual Sunraysia Desert Rally is fairly typical, being an extremely popular, well run and rapidly growing promotion. In the 1973 event, 311 motorcycles and 79 four wheelers (cars and buggies) took part. The cars had to tackle a 96 km (60 mile) circuit of rough countryside; the bikes, which are superior to cars for this kind of work, had a 144 km (90 mile) circuit of even rougher terrain reaching out over the sandy desert scrub and salt pan country south of Mildura, Victoria.

Top: *Camera angles dramatise action but even so these Montesa moto-cross machines are really storming the heights.*

Bottom left: *Hitting the hay with a Montesa Trail.*
Bottom right: *The atmosphere of an action packed meet.*

The event is specially popular with riders because highly specialised machinery is not required. Twenty-five different brands were represented in 1973, classified into trail (without knobby tyres), scramble and enduro cycles. The first two classes were further subdivided into 125 cm³, 250 and unlimited sections, while enduros were subdivided into classes above and below 200 cm³.

It was a great race with spills galore, the only serious injury being a broken ankle.

Outright winner was veteran Victorian scrambler, Bob Walpole, riding a 400 cm³ Husqvana. He picked up $700 prize money. Runner-up for outright honours was Melbourne student Stephen Cramer on a Honda 250. All competitors had a thrilling ride, the route being summed up beautifully by one competitor, Wayne Cantrell, as follows:—

'A short dirt track, a rutted curve, two small hillocks then up and over the crest of a hill — airborne for a few seconds before plummeting down the other side. A sharp left turn, then 300 yards of suspension smashing humps and hollows before dropping over the lip of a big salt pan. A quick burst across the end of the lake, into the hard uphill right hand turn and on to the soft deep sand and spindly Mallee bush.'

If this kind of riding is your thing, you'll love enduro riding.

GRASS AND SHORT CIRCUIT RACING

Both are variations of speedway riding, on open ground. There are no right hand bends in grass track racing, whereas short circuit events include left and right hand bends.

Originally short circuit racing in Australia was called Miniature TT though in postwar years the name went out of use. Track surfaces are relatively smooth. Each lap is less than 1.6 km (1 mile) in length, there being anything from four to 12 laps to one race. On some circuits speeds up to 144 kmh (90 mph) are possible but other circuits are tighter so speeds are far slower. Riders leave the starting line bunched together, as in speedway riding, and the first to reach the first corner has a useful advantage.

Four-stroke engines have an edge for grass and short circuit racing in the higher capacity classes, Hagon-JAP machines being especially popular, whereas two stroke designs, such as Bultaco and Montesa dominate the smaller capacity classes.

Championship events draw up to 300 entries and 2000 spectators, with prize money up to $150 for a title win.

SPEEDWAY RIDING

The spectacular nature of the racing and the excellent spectator amenities at many stadiums consistently result in large crowds. The record figure, currently held by Claremont Speedway in Perth, is 38,000 spectators. Rowley Park, Adelaide; Brisbane's Exhibition Ground; Sydney's Showground; Premier Speedway, Warrnambool and Tralee Speedway, Canberra — also draw consistently large crowds.

Speedway riding had its origins 'down under' in the early 1920's. Australian ace Billy Galloway then introduced the sport to Britain in 1928. His thrilling displays of broadslides astonished spectators and would-be-competitors alike, launching the new sport in a blaze of enthusiasm. Waves of Australian riders went overseas, demonstrating and competing. By 1935 there were 50 speedway tracks operating in Britain alone and the sport spread rapidly across Europe.

An interesting fact about solo speedway racing bikes is that they always travel anti-clockwise around the track. Also they are probably the only type of wheeled racing machines which do not have brakes.

The first world championship was held in 1936, with competitors from 10 countries. Lionel van Praag, then Australia's leading rider, became the first world champion after a series of hard fought run-offs. Today twenty or more Australian riders jet to Britain each year for the speedway season. Their skill is held in high regard. The current world champion, Ivan Mauger, is a New Zealander, and few are better known on the international scene than New Zealander Barry Briggs, four times world champion.

Australian speedway circuits tend to be much longer than their European counterparts, so different riding techniques and speeds are necessary. This tends to put local riders at a disadvantage when competing overseas, but our top riders are unquestionably world class, especially men like Johnny Boulger, Jim Airey, Billy Sanders, John Langfield and Phil Crump.

There are more than 120 circuits in Australia, of which 29 feature solo riding. Ten of the 23 tracks in New Zealand feature solos. Nearly 500 regular solo competitors take part in the 38 week summer season in the two countries. Not all hit the big money, of course, but A0 grade riders can command $150 or more a night. Top drawcards double this sum and more. Ivan Mauger for example, is paid $1000 to appear at top Australian tracks.

One reason why the future of the sport is assured is that a unique experiment has met with staggering success. In 1972, the Brisbane Exhibition Ground began a season of junior league, for people 17 years and up, racing against each other before the evening's main events. The standard of riding quickly rose to the point where the top four 'juniors' each night were invited to mix in with the professionals during the main events.

RALLIES
Rallies are non-competitive outings in which riders join for a convivial weekend to relax, yarn about cycling and enjoy themselves. Such events take many forms, but typical is the popular Alpine Rally organised annually in NSW. The 1973 event was held at Yarrangobilly, 20 miles from Kiandra. More than 500 riders converged from places as far afield as West Australia and Northern Queensland, travelling prescribed routes to attend the rally and weekend camp-out. One especially keen traveller came 700 miles on a minibike!

RECORD BREAKING
It takes more than nerve and suitable equipment to break a speed record. A suitable track and ideal weather conditions are imperative. As record speeds rise, so does the importance of the track. At three figure speeds, a gust of wind or a bump in the surface can throw the machine off course and possibly out of control.

Speed records are counted only when timed by an official body who take the mean of two runs in opposite directions, thus averaging out any advantage from wind or slope.

At the time of writing the world speed record for a two-wheeler is 425 kmh (262.5 mph) held by a Harley Davidson streamliner, ridden by Cal Rayborn.

Australia's record speed is more modest — 245 kmh (150.3 mph) held by Bryan Hindle of Sydney on a 350 cm³ Yamaha. Yamaha, in fact, hold a flock of records, established by Hindle and Brian Collins at Lake LeFroy in West Australia. They also clocked 111 kmh (69.51 mph) with a 30 cm³ model 133 kmh (108.61 mph) with a 125 cm³ bike.

Sydney rider, Bob Sharp, hopes to be the first Australian to top 324 kmh (200 mph). A well-known drag racing champion and speedway rider, he has constructed a twin Triumph engined special with supercharged nitro fuelled twin engines which, he hopes, will exceed the 'double ton' on the dry salt pan flats at Lake LeFroy.

Potentially the world's fastest machine is the Honda Hawk, built in the USA geared for 480 kmh (300 mph). During 1972 it crashed in a record attempt, having achieving 265 kmh (290 mph) in one direction and travelling at an estimated 430 kmh (270 mph) in the opposite direction when it unaccountably went out of control and crashed. It is now being rebuilt with twin Honda 750 cm³ racing engines each capable of developing 150 bhp.

RACING COLOUR CODE:

Australia used the international system of colour coding racing motorcycles as follows:—

SOLO MOTORCYCLES

		Classification
Up to 50 ccs	— White background, black numbers	—
51-125 ccs	— Green background, white numbers	Ultra-lightweight
126-250 ccs	— Green background, white numbers	Lightweight
251-350 ccs	— Blue background, white numbers	Junior
351-500 ccs	— Yellow background, black numbers	Senior
351-1300 ccs	— Yellow background, black numbers	Unlimited

SIDE-CARS

Up to 650 ccs	— White background, black numbers	Junior
651-1300 ccs	— Yellow background, black numbers	Senior

Top: *All the excitement of two-wheeled racing in Australia is captured in this dramatic start.*

Bottom: *Short circuit racing makes excellent spectator sport. Here Keith Davies (No 297) leads Peter Collins (No 59) with former Australian champion Bill McDonald just behind but obscured from view. Taken at Amaroo Park.*

Top left: *Jim Airey, top Australian contender, shows the art of speedway riding.*

Top right: *Geoff Leighton shows his form as he wins the 1972 Sunraysia Desert Rally, riding a 250 Kawasaki.*

Bottom: *Brian Collins congratulates Bryan Hindle after he has set a new 350 cm³ Australian record, riding a Yamaha. His speed was more than 150 mph (240 kmh).*

OFF ROADING ROCKS, RIVERS AND ROUGH STUFF

When it comes to experiencing what motorcycling is all about, nothing compares with riding off the beaten track.

There is a sense of adventure, exhilarating freedom and the challenge of pitting your skill against unpredictable Mother Nature. You learn to tackle and conquer terrain ranging from muddy hillsides to hard rutted surfaces, from creek crossings to long grass with the occasional hidden pothole.

Off-road enthusiasts are countless. Some are content to explore new places, roaming the countryside at large; others prefer the competitive stimulus of moto-cross, enduro, sporting trials or off-road racing.

Off the road, you'll find a wide assortment of ages and occupations—girls, boys, housewives, tradesmen, professional men and business executives. Once they have donned helmet, boots, goggles and riding suit, they become as one.

Moto-cross and sporting trials are competitive events where skill is the deciding factor, but it all starts with trail riding. For this is where the basic skills of concentration, control and judgment are learned.

No one knows the origin of trail riding as a recreation but it probably started in Australia. Hundreds of motorcycles were used on Australian country properties before the second world war, and their riders soon discovered they were as useful for filling in leisure hours as for boundary riding.

After the second world war, Spanish factories began to specialise in off-road bikes, concentrating on competition machines. Japanese firms began production and saw the future of dual purpose designs, suitable for road and trail. To this end they made a series of compromises in gearing, power, tyre treads and suspension. The riding position was midway between a comfortable roadster and a stand-on-the pegs trials machine, but the results were good. Genuinely versatile machines, suitable for commuting to work or hitting the hills, became an accepted part of the scene.

The trend today is to machines specifically designed for off-road work, though some excellent dual purpose designs are still built. Australian buyers can choose between 70 different off-roaders. Half are trail bikes, 27 moto-cross or sporting trial designs and there's a handful of enduros. Models range from 50 cm³ minitrail bikes to 400 cm³ heavyweights, though the main action is in the 150-250 cm³ class.

An increasing number of sporting trials and outright off-road scramblers are seen, though many are used purely for pleasure

riding, rather than competition. Some astute observers believe that the future of the motorcycle industry lies in trail and off-road machines and that in the years to come many companies will concentrate in this direction.

Already there is a marked exodus from cities to the bush at weekends — a trend as strong in USA and Europe as in Australia and New Zealand. Unfortunately there are fewer and fewer areas near major cities where off-roaders are permitted, though special riding parks are now being set aside for this purpose.

As a result, riders are seeking as much action and enjoyment as possible in relatively confined areas. A sporting trial, either impromptu or organised, is the easiest way to pack a lot of action in a small space, which is why so many firms are developing sporting trial designs.

Long distance trail riding is still possible, but such treks are being made at increasing distances from major cities. Fortunately, some excellent riding parks have opened. One example is a 2000 hectare (5000 acre) riding property between Parkes and Wellington, NSW — 550 kms (220 miles) west of Sydney.

More official riding areas are expected in all States, especially with the establishment of the Australian Motorcycle Trail Riders Association (AMTRA). Its main aim is to encourage trail riding and help enthusiasts enjoy it to the full. The address of your State branch should be available from a nearby motorcycle dealer specialising in off-roading.

AMTRA and similar bodies organise outings well away from populated areas, with well marked routes involving gravel roads, forest tracks and a variety of interesting terrain.

Trail riding can be done year round, in all kinds of weather and by riders of all ages. Apart from a suitable machine, all you need is proper clothing — light and comfortable helmet, goggles, strong knee length boots, gloves, pants and jacket. Many experienced riders prefer the popular Belstaff trails riding suit, which is strong and waterproof.

Bikes must be registered and properly silenced for AMTRA events. Most treks are completed in one day but camping weekends are organised from time to time.

Whether organised by a club or not, a trail ride should be undertaken as part of a group — in the interest of safety as well as companionship. In remote areas, a minimum of three machines is desirable. Should a rider get hurt, there is always someone to stay with him while a third goes for help. With larger groups, there should be a lead man and a tail man and, if both know their job, the party stays together at all times.

An advantage of club outings is that the trails are often clearly marked. Distances covered range from 80 kms (50 miles) for beginners to 160 kms (100 miles) for experienced riders. The routes are planned so the riders are back at base before dark. Even complete newcomers can enjoy such outings. It is worth knowing that many clubs hold school days for beginners, in which riding techniques, preparation of machines and the finer points of following a trail are outlined. Other activities include navigation trials, enduros, field days and social nights where riders swap yarns which sometimes tend to be as expansive as some fishermen's tales!

State aerial survey maps are extremely useful for trail riding, especially the topographical type, but to know the best general areas for riding, it is essential to make contact with keen off-roaders. The eastern half of NSW for example is a trail rider's paradise if you know where to look.

Of special interest is the 180 kms (100 miles) between Sydney and Newcastle and the 105 kms (65 miles) between Sydney and Katoomba. Old roads and tracks built by convict labour a century ago still exist — some in surprisingly good condition. In other States there are equally attractive riding areas for those with local knowledge.

Experienced trail riders carry plenty of fuel and refreshment (especially water), as well as a well chosen selection of spare parts and tools. They know too that when a track passes through private property, riders should call at the homestead and ask permission to proceed. Refusal is rare — provided that the riders are not carrying firearms.

OFF ROAD RIDING TECHNIQUES

A knowledge of basic techniques, plus plenty of practice is a sure path to expert riding. Many enthusiasts begin with a minicycle, which is easy to transport, light to manhandle when bogged and simple to ride. Heavier machines need more ex-

perience when handling tricky conditions, but there is no reason why a beginner should not start with almost any kind of off-roader.

It is best to practise on soft ground. Almost certainly you will take a spill — many in fact — but no harm should result provided you travel at a sensible speed and wear the right gear. Even so, it is prudent to travel with a friend when practising and leave word at home what time you can be expected back.

Find a suitable stretch of grass, free of concealed pot holes if possible and start by riding in tight circles. You'll quickly appreciate the importance of throttle control. Grab a handful of revs and you'll almost certainly cause the rear wheel to spin or the front wheel to leave the ground, so finesse is essential. Concentration and delicate accelerator control are basic elements of off-roading, so do not proceed to other techniques until you can feed in just enough power to keep the bike rolling at a steady speed on a very slippery surface.

Next practise riding while standing on the foot pegs. Use your weight to guide the bike, swaying it from side to side, while you remain upright. You soon find that you can accurately steer the machine this way, and if you line up a few rocks, you can try weaving in and out of them.

The next step is to try your hand on a variety of different surfaces, learning how the machine reacts to the accelerator and brakes. The more slippery the surface, the harder the bike is to control, so plenty of practice is needed. Should you find the bike sliding from under you, simply step off and mark it down as another lesson learned. No-one ever became a good off-roader the easy way, so don't feel too put down when you take a spill.

You will also find that a slide can be made to work FOR you, especially on tight corners.

To set up a slide, approach a tight turn at a modest speed and lock the rear wheel with a touch of the foot brake. The back of the bike will start to slide outwards and when this happens ease off the brake pressure. You can control the degree of slide by turning the front wheel in the same direction that the back wheel is sliding. With practice it becomes possible to broadside around a very tight bend with a neat

movement, controlled by the amount of power and the angle you turn the front wheel in the direction of the slide.

Should an unintentional slide occur at any time, ease off the throttle and don't touch either brake, otherwise the slide will become worse. If the slide continues when the power is shut off, simply turn the front wheel a little in the same direction.

BRAKING ON SOFT SURFACES
As we saw earlier in the book, the easiest way to cause an unintentional slide is to hit the brakes too hard and lock up a wheel. This is easily done on a slippery surface, and once a wheel is sliding, you have little control. A rolling tyre always has more grip on the ground than a sliding one, so use the brakes gingerly, and ease off pressure if either wheel starts to slide.

To practise this technique, find a suitable soft surface away from trees and rocks and make a series of stops using the front brake only. You'll soon find how much pressure you can apply without locking the wheel — and how to ease off and reapply pressure, halting the bike without sliding a wheel. Make a similar series of stops with the rear brake only, then repeat using both brakes simultaneously.

Braking on a slippery surface is such a vital part of off-road riding that you must thoroughly master it before trying other techniques.

WHEELIES
Flicking the front wheel in the air may look like the stunt of a young kid but it can be surprisingly useful for riding over fallen trees or unavoidable small rocks. It is also invaluable when climbing very sharp banks where the frame might otherwise hit the ground as you come over the top.

A wheelie is not achieved by speed but is the result of torque and balance. It can be achieved from a standing start, at a walking pace or at faster speeds. To practise, stand on the foot pegs while riding slowly in low gear. Crack open the throttle and lean backwards. This brings up the front wheel, the height depending on the power and how far back you lean. With continued practice, you learn to execute a wheelie, raising the front wheel to exactly the required height.

ROUGH ROADS

Rocky terrain is especially hard on tyres and wheels. It pays to keep the tyre pressures firm to minimise blows on the wheel rims and also to travel slowly. Knobby tyres offer much less grip on rocks than conventional tyres, so ride accordingly, otherwise you might easily take a bruising fall. A low, low gear and plenty of control are needed for tackling very rocky surfaces.

Rutted roads also present a problem. Sometimes the front wheel gets caught in one rut, the rear wheel in another and there's no way to keep control.

To avoid ruts, rocks and other problems, stand on the foot pegs and shift the bike from side to side, dodging the obstructions. The faster you travel, the more important this becomes. You may know that desert racers weave the bike underneath them like a living thing, dodging obstacles they could not possibly ride around in the normal way.

ROCKS AND FALLEN TREES

A quick way of wrecking the front end is to hit rocks or fallen trees. You might also take a spill. Rocks are very hard on man and machine, so travel slowly, ready to take evasive action when necessary. If you cannot steer around an obstacle, either stop or raise the front wheel and ride over it. Having committed yourself to tackling one big rock, look ahead immediately in case there is another directly in front.

The standard way of getting over a fallen tree is to lift the front wheel high enough to pass over without touching, but even if you do not get this high, the wheelie will at least minimise the impact. Keep the throttle open after lifting the front as you want the back wheel to climb over the tree. As it does so, keep your weight back so that you land rear wheel first on the other side of the tree. This is not always possible but very desirable. Front wheel landings are bad — because of the impact on the front forks and because you cannot be sure whether the cycle will continue straight ahead or (more likely) fold over and throw you across the handlebars.

Experts can climb over trees or rocks as much as 910 mm (3 ft) in diameter, but most of us are content with less ambitious climbs. If necessary, stop and man-handle the machine over the heavy stuff, another reason why it pays to ride in groups.

BANKS

Steep banks, especially muddy ones, present a unique problem. Whether going up or down, the basic technique requires balance and accelerator control. When coming down, first select the path offering the most traction and least grade. Select a low gear, stand on the pegs and ride down without touching the brakes, if possible. A fairly slow speed is often necessary, otherwise you might slam the front wheel into the ground as you come off the bank.

When you want to ride up a bank, there is often insufficient traction to start the climb, so it is necessary to gain a little speed and lift the front wheel as you approach. Keep the power on, and climb fairly briskly, coming over the top with the front wheel still in the air. This prevents the middle of the frame grounding as you go over the top. Once the rear wheel is over, close the accelerator. This brings down the front wheel and slows down the bike while you reassess the line you wish to follow.

RIDING UPHILL

An almost infinite number of different types of grades can be found off the road, so no single technique works in all cases. Basically, traction is the key to climbing a steep grade because the bike quickly stops when the rear wheel loses its grip. To get maximum traction you need as much weight over the back wheel as possible. On the other hand, when too much weight is taken off the front, there is a chance that the bike will do a backwards loop!

If the front wheel starts to rise off the ground, lean forward a little and shut off the throttle a trifle. The extra weight and deceleration brings the front wheel down to earth. The secret of climbing really steep hills is to practise balance and accelerator control to the point where you achieve maximum rear wheel traction with minimum front wheel lift.

Remember that too much throttle may cause the rear wheel to spin or — if the tyre digs into the ground — cause the front wheel to lift off the ground.

A little thought goes a long way. Consider whether to climb straight up the hillside, or zig-zag so as to lessen the grade. Maybe you should even go around the back of the hill and look for a better ascent!

On long hills, use just enough power to maintain a steady speed. Choose the gear ratio which best suits the grade — first gear is not necessarily the best, especially on slippery surfaces. Remember that if it is necessary to rush a short sharp hill, be ready to back off the accelerator when going over the top. Apart from speeding into the unknown, an open throttle may keep the front wheel in the air a lot longer than you want it there.

RIDING DOWNHILL

It is often more difficult to come down a steep hill than go up it, so obviously it pays to figure out the best approach before starting. Having decided on the line to follow, sit well back (or stand on the pegs and lean back), coming down slowly in low gear. If engine braking is not enough to control your speed, use the rear brake only — and gently. As you near the bottom of the hill, look for a suitable run off point that will lesser the impact of the level ground on the front forks.

Should it be obvious that a hill is too steep or slippery to ride down, don't be a hero. Look for another path. But if you do get caught on a too-steep hill and find the bike running away with you, a ready means of escape is to stamp on the rear brake, swing the bike around and lay it down, with you

and the bike facing uphill. With lighter machines especially this is is a practical way of avoiding uncontrolled downhill runs.

The next step is to walk the bike down — bull-dogging as it is called. Kill the engine, engage first gear and pull in the clutch lever. This way you have extra braking control should the bike want to run downhill — just let out the clutch lever to slow it down.

As you proceed downhill, dig your feet into the dirt or ground, as though coming down a steep snow drift. Take your time, work down the grade and avoid the muddiest patches.

SAND

The basic rule in soft sand is to sit well back in the saddle and turn on the power. The rear wheel may tend to spin a lot but this is sometimes necessary to keep going. If, however, the bike won't keep on the move, jump off, keep the engine running, engage first gear and walk beside it with the engine doing the work. If this does not get you through — practically nothing will!

One problem with sand is that the tyre types make little difference — traction is the problem with any kind of tyre.

MUD

Like sand, mud presents a traction problem but in this case, tyres make a big difference. Knobby tyres especially seem to find some way of gripping.

To tackle mud, the technique is to ride slowly, using second or third gear, with a steady accelerator opening. You want the minimum power necessary to keep the bike on the move. Opening the accelerator even a notch too much will cause the rear wheel to spin in the mud. Progress will stop.

Keep the front wheel pointing directly ahead unless you have to make a turn — in which case follow the widest curve possible. Try to avoid stopping until you hit firm ground. Starting from rest in mud is often the most difficult part. Once underway, be content to move slowly and smoothly — a bike can slide from under you as quickly as a toboggan.

CREEK CROSSINGS

Where water depth is concerned, never guess. Even if it means wading through the water, you must know its exact maximum depth. Should the engine gulp in water you could expect a bent connecting rod at the very least. It is, therefore, unwise to attempt to ride through any water coming above the level of the exhaust pipe, air cleaner or electrical equipment.

Where the water level is safe, proceed as though riding through mud, using first gear and the minimum accelerator to maintain a steady walking pace. Don't try to lift your legs clear of the water — it might be hard enough to balance the machine in the normal way without this extra complication.

Once the water is crossed, dry out the brakes by riding some distance while applying the front and rear brake levers. This will build up heat within the brake drums, driving off the water. As soon as the brakes respond normally, the linings are dry and will work normally.

JUMPING

Though some spectacular jumping manoeuvres can be done by experts, it is as well to remember that trail bikes are not bucking broncos. A smashed front fork (or broken rider) is a common penalty for a mistake.

The key points of jumping are these. Keep the front wheel pointing straight ahead, before, during and immediately after the jump; make sure that the rear wheel touches the ground before the front wheel.

Obviously balance plays an important part because if the front wheel hits the ground first, there is no knowing how the bike would react. So when approaching a jump, open the throttle, as the extra power tends to lift the front wheel a little. The bike becomes airborne while still accelerating, then by keeping your weight backwards make sure that the front wheel stays higher than the back wheel for the whole jump. After touch-down, leave the brakes alone until full steering control is regained.

The prudent rider starts with small jumps, working up to bigger things only as his experience, confidence and knowledge grow.

Indeed, this last sentence sums up the whole key to successful, enjoyable off-road riding.

SIZZLING SUPERBIKES

Since the dawn of motorcycling there have been special high performance machines, with braking and handling qualities to match.

In recent years such designs have sold in large numbers, producing a class now known as Superbike.

What constitutes a superbike is open to debate but it is generally accepted that the class is reserved for motorcycles with engine capacities of 650 cm³ and more. Such machines can comfortably out-accelerate a 12-cylinder Jaguar, many having a higher top speed than the lastest Mercedes V-8. Surprisingly, a superbike can be more economical on fuel than a mini sedan.

The bare specifications may conjure up a vision of a big, brutally powerful machine with little to commend it except sizzling acceleration. But most designs are highly civilised touring machines, quiet, superbly comfortable on long trips and as easy to handle as a lightweight roadster.

They are the two wheeled equivalent of the Grand Touring muscle car, with an outstanding performance, matched by superior braking, steering and road manners. Skilful riders know how to use the power to accelerate out of trouble, when necessary, while the tenacious road holding is a positive safety factor.

One of the first real superbikes was the Vincent Black Shadow Series B, designed by Australia's Phil Irving, who was later noted for the world beating Repco-Brabham Formula One V-8 racing engine. Irving was chief designer at the HRD concern in Britain immediately after the second world war when he produced the Black Shadow and Black Lightning series. In 1947 the Black Shadow Series B had a 998 cm³ twin cylinder engine developing 56 hp at 5800 rpm. The timed top speed was 200 kmh (122 mph) and it could turn the standing quarter mile (400 metres) into history in 15.1 seconds.

Compared with the figures in our chart, Black Shadow was impressively rapid, even by today's standards. The big difference was its price. It took more than one year's average wage to buy one, whereas a tradesman mechanic can now buy an equivalent machine with 15 weeks' wages.

After the modern superbike appeared in 1968 the class quickly established itself and soon began to boom. During 1973 some Australian distributors reported sales were far greater than they had anticipated. One sold 220 superbikes in a single month, many found that superbikes were beginning to outsell much cheaper, lighter models.

Despite fuel consumption between 40 and 70 miles per gallon (4.5 to 7 litres per 100 km), superbikes are not cheap to run. Average registration costs in NSW run to $70 a year, with comprehensive insurance showing little change from $200. Fortunately the designs are very durable, apart from rear tyres and chains, which seldom last for more than a few thousand kilometres, especially when the rider makes full use of the available performance.

Most are amazingly docile when handled gently, with quiet exhaust notes and a high degree of refinement. They snap to life only when the rider commands.

The 'slowest' superbike is good for 180 kmh (110 mph) but maximum speed potential is of academic interest only, because there are few places left in Australia where high speeds are legal. The speed of these machines is really the by-product of the tremendous power made

Kawasaki 900.

available for rapid acceleration and fuss-free cruising. Many superbikes have five gears and, in top, can cruise at 114 kmh (70 mph) with the engine humming cheerfully at less than 5000 rpm.

An exciting thing about the superbike class is that buyers choose from a wide range of engineering philosophies. Engine designs include gutsy V-twins and smooth vertical fours, a water cooled two-stroke and an air cooled three cylinder four-stroke. Power outputs range from 40 to 67 kw (53 to 90 hp), vehicle weights from 195 to 358 kg (425 to 791 lbs). The bikes themselves are not especially big, typical dimensions being 2220 mm (87 ins) long, 1320 mm (52 ins) wide, 1140 mm (45 ins) high, 1530 mm (60 in) wheelbase and 157 mm (6.3 ins) ground clearance. At low speeds it takes strong wrists and ankles to manoeuvre the big bikes, but once under way they seem to shed their weight and establish perfect balance.

Sophisticated design features include disc brakes front and rear for Harley Davidson; automatic lube system for Kawasaki's chain; shaft drive (BMW and Guzzi) and independent injected lubrication for Suzuki's two-stroke engine. Other interesting features include a tyre wear indicator, a warning lamp which glows when the

brake linings wear down and an indicator light to show when neutral gear is selected.

Perhaps the most sensational superbike yet is the Munch Mammoth. The brainchild of a self-taught engineering genius, Friedl Munch, of Germany, the huge machine has an NSU car engine in its frame. The four cylinder 1177 cm³ air cooled overhead camshaft unit develops 95 hp even before tweaking and with optional fuel injection develops 125 hp. Extensive use is made of alloy to keep down overall weight. Despite fairly high gearing to permit an incredible 268 kmh (167 mph) top speed, acceleration is extremely rapid.

Correctly the Munch is called the TTS, not the Mammoth, the latter being a nickname for wishful thinkers. If superbikes are the stuff your dreams are made of, these additional notes will fire your fantasies.

BMW R75/5

Accepted as one of the best engineered motorcycles ever built, the BMW R75/5 is powered by a horizontal four-stroke twin cylinder engine delivering 57 well nourished horsepower. The German firm has traditionally used shaft drive to the rear wheel, thus eliminating the major bugbear of superbike travel — rapid chain wear. Extensive use of light alloys keeps overall weight down to a manageable 195 kg (430 lbs). Electric starter, surprisingly comfortable suspension and tenacious handling transform the R75/5 into a living legend.

DUCATI GT 750
Built in Italy, this lightweight superbike is noted for its powerful brakes, excellent handling and unusually flexible engine. The forward leaning V-twin four-stroke has the capacity to remain cool and unruffled after the hardest imaginable riding. The design is intended more as a fast touring machine than a competition bike and is agile enough to bring pleasure to suburban riding.

HARLEY DAVIDSON ELECTRAGLIDE
Flagship of the American fleet and one of the heaviest cycles of all time, Superglide hits the showroom floor at more than $3000. Highly extrovert in appearance, its abundant chrome, colourful stripes and white wall tyres would stand out, even in a parking lot of superbikes. The biggest and heaviest, weighing nearly 356 kg (800 lbs), it is naturally dubbed the Yank Tank. There is, however, nothing sluggish about its acceleration nor its ability to cruise almost indefinitely at high speeds.

The weight problem eliminates the use of a centre stand and the rider learns to keep the machine almost vertical when manoeuvring. The huge vee engine has massive torque at low speeds and pulls with the determination of a locomotive. The stopping department is capably looked after by disc brakes front and rear, with hydraulic operation.

HONDA CB 750
The best seller in the class, Honda's 750 'four' is remarkably quiet and refined, combining a fuss-free temperament with uncanny smoothness and potent urgency. The beautifully designed light alloy four cylinder engine has a single overhead camshaft with a fairly flat power curve, reducing the need to change gears in the lower speed ranges. Well priced, it is a highly civilised Japanese import with a brisker performance than many sports cars costing 10 times the price. A feature of the CB 750 is the complete absence of vibration. Even the rear vision mirror remains rock steady at speed.

KAWASAKI 900
A superbike among superbikes, Kawasaki has a large overhead cam four cylinder four-stroke delivering 82 horses with complete smoothness. Capable of speeds up to 208 kmh (130 mph), with stopping power to match, it can be ridden around town with remarkable ease. It is also the most powerful production cycle made in Japan.

On the open road, big K proves an extremely rapid tourer, capable of pulling

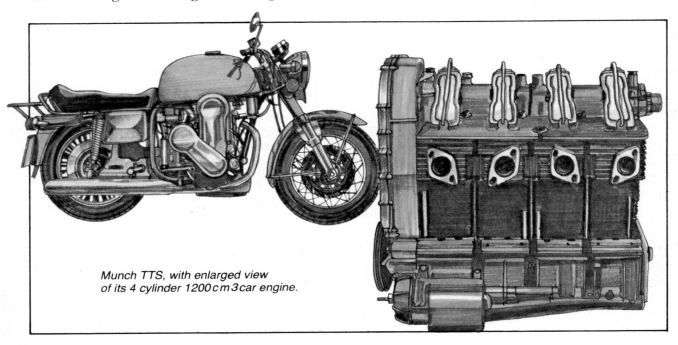

Munch TTS, with enlarged view of its 4 cylinder 1200 cm3 car engine.

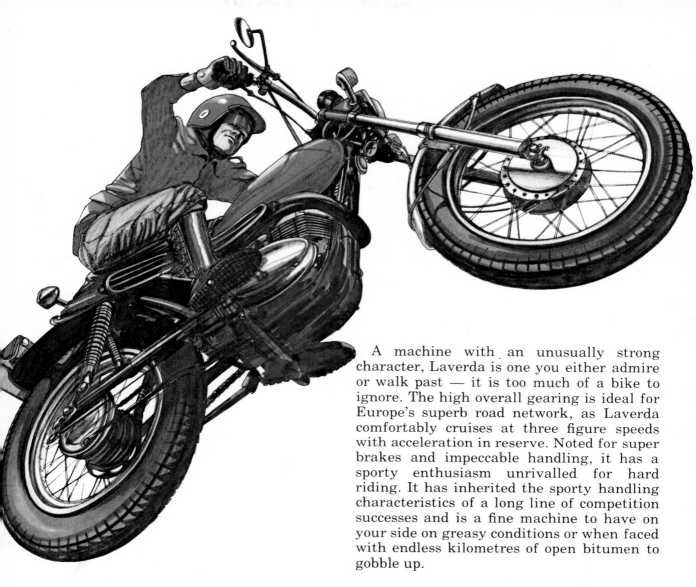

A machine with an unusually strong character, Laverda is one you either admire or walk past — it is too much of a bike to ignore. The high overall gearing is ideal for Europe's superb road network, as Laverda comfortably cruises at three figure speeds with acceleration in reserve. Noted for super brakes and impeccable handling, it has a sporty enthusiasm unrivalled for hard riding. It has inherited the sporty handling characteristics of a long line of competition successes and is a fine machine to have on your side on greasy conditions or when faced with endless kilometres of open bitumen to gobble up.

from walking pace in top gear and winding up to three figure speeds in a few seconds. Thanks to a five speed gearbox with overdrive top, it can cruise at 112 kmh (70 mph) with the engine almost loafing at 4500 rpm.

The 900 established itself in Australia on its first competitive outing, during a production bike race in Adelaide. Victorian riders John Crawford and Mick Hone beat a brace of Honda 750's to take outright honours.

LAVERDA 750
Made in Italy with rare sculptured elegance, the five-speed Laverda 750 is cast in a different mould from most in the class — being unashamedly an open road high performance go-mobile for the man who does not mind a temperamental handful in the city.

MOTO GUZZI V7
Though big and powerful, this Italian import is easier to handle than its weight suggests. Thanks to superb balance, it can be flicked on to its centre stand as readily as a lightweight. Once rolling, the rider forgets about the weight to concentrate on the impressive engineering and glorious road manners. Quiet and smooth, V7 handles like a dream, on smooth roads and under adverse conditions, taking sharp bends as though the tyres were sticky and precisely obeying the rider's every whim.

Like BMW, Guzzi has a shaft drive to eliminate chain wear problems. The 64 hp twin cylinder four-stroke gives a maximum speed of 200 kmh (125 mph) with astonishing fuel economy. An Australian owner completed a 2920 km (1825 mile) touring trip, averaging 4.1 litres per 100 km (73 mpg).

MV AGUSTA 750S

One of Italy's top eliminators, MV Agusta has been well publicised as the ideal complement to the riding genius of champion Giacomo Agostini. One of the most powerful machines made anywhere, it has a beautifully built four cylinder four-stroke that revs to astronomical heights without a trace of vibration. Maximum power comes in at 7900 rpm, but the engine also pulls smoothly from 2000 rpm.

Surprisingly, the successful factory is virtually the hobby of helicopter millionaire Count Dominica Agusta, which is why some of the world's best riders are in its racing stable, rewriting motorcycle racing history.

The road-going version looks little different from other superbikes, but it costs twice as much, being virtually a hand-built pedigree product. Possibly the most exclusive road going machine a rider can own, it has just about the best road manners in the world.

NORTON COMMANDO

Big things are expected from the Norton-Villiers group now they have acquired BSA-Triumph.

Well priced and capable of tremendously rapid transport, Commando inherits a long history of competition success. Design-wise, it is unusual. The four stroke OHV parallel twin engine, four speed transmission and swinging arm rear suspension are attached to a patented revolutionary frame in which the main components are isolated by rubber mounts. The result is a very smooth and brisk acceleration.

Another advantage is the relatively light weight — only 195 kg (430 lbs). In February 1973, at Santa Pod Drag Strip, England, a Commando 850, silenced to conform with stringent Californian laws and ridden by a company test rider, was electronically timed over the standing quarter mile (400 m) at 12.52 seconds. The terminal speed was 167 kmh (104 mph). That's what Commando riding is all about.

Model	Approximate Price	0-97 kmh 0-60 mph Acceleration	¼ mile (400 metres) Acceleration	0-160 kmh 0-100 mph Acceleration	Top speed	Engine capacity in cm³	Engine	Factory claimed horsepower	Weight
BMW R75/5	$2,000	4.9 secs	14.6 secs	16.0 secs	113 mph 178 kmh	745	Horizontal twin four-stroke	57 at 6400 rpm 42.5 kw	430 lbs 195 kg
DUCATI GT 750	$1,700	4.8 secs	12.7 secs	—	123 mph 197 kmh	748	Vee twin four-stroke	58 at 7000 rpm 43.5 kw	425 lbs 193 kg
HARLEY-DAVIDSON Electraglide	$3,200	7.7 secs	15.6 secs	15.6 secs	112 mph 177 kmh	1200	Vee twin four-stroke OHV	65 at 6200 rpm 48.5 kw	791 lbs 360 kg
HONDA CB 750	$1,650	4.4 secs	—	12.0 secs	119 mph 191 kmh	736	Four cylinder four-stroke	65 at 8000 rpm 48.5 kw	515 lbs 233 kg
KAWASAKI 900	$1,900	—	12.2 secs	—	130 mph 208 kmh	903	Four-stroke DOHC four cylinder	82 at 8500 rpm 61 kw	520 lbs 235 kg
LAVERDA 750 SF	$1,850	4.9 secs	—	15.8 secs	116 mph 185 kmh	744	Twin cylinder four-stroke OHV	60 at 7000 rpm 45 kw	510 lbs 230 kg
MOTO GUZZI V7	$2,150	6.0 secs	13.8 secs	12.5 secs	129 mph 207 kmh	844	Vee twin four-stroke	64 at 6500 rpm 48 kw	530 lbs 240 kg
MUNCH	Not available	4.0 secs	12.1 secs	11.1 secs	167 mph 268 kmh	1177	Four cylinder air cooled transverse	125 at 8000 rpm 93 kw	565 lbs 255 kg
M.V. AGUSTA	$4,000	5.4 secs	13.9 secs	13.8 secs	122 mph 195 kmh	743	Four cylinder DOHC four-stroke	60 at 7900 rpm 45 kw	515 lbs 233 kg
NORTON COMMANDO	$1,800	4.3 secs	12.5 secs	12.9 secs	125 mph 200 kmh	828	Vertical twin OHV four-stroke	65 at 5900 rpm 48.5 kw	430 lbs 195 kg
SUZUKI 750 GT	$1,550	6.2 secs	—	19.1 secs	110 mph 176 kmh	738	Water cooled two-stroke three cylinder	67 at 6500 rpm 50 kw	510 lbs 230 kg
TRIUMPH TRIDENT	$1,850	6.0 secs	—	13.2 secs	122 mph 195 kmh	740	Three cylinder four-stroke	63 at 7500 rpm 47 kw	485 lbs 220 kg
YAMAHA TX 750	$1,450	4.9 secs	13.2 secs	—	105 mph 168 kmh	743	SOHC four-stroke, parallel twin	63 at 5700 rpm 47 kw	463 lbs 211 kg

SUZUKI 750 GT

The only machine in its class with a water cooled two-stroke engine, Suzuki seems to have eliminated the problem of large capacity two-stroke design, while retaining the traditional advantages. Water cooling helps dampen the noise as well as removing any tendency for the central cylinder to over-heat. A two-stroke 'three' has a similar firing rhythm to a four-stroke six, so it is no surprise to learn that the big Suzuki is about the smoothest in the business. Without a trace of vibration, it revs with such abandon that it is freqently compared with a Wankel rotary.

Electric starting, loads of low speed torque and superb top gear flexibility make it a highly civilised tourer, though there is searing acceleration when required. The 750 GT is noted for its comfortable suspension and riding refinement.

TRIUMPH TRIDENT 750

Another three cylinder machine, this British design has a four-stroke air cooled engine, developed through a highly successful racing program, campaigning in production and formula races. Specifications include triple carburettors and a front disc brake. The five-speed gearbox has the ratios closely spaced to give a surge of power from 4000 to more than 8000 rpm. The suspension is set up for high speed, open road riding but it is a machine that can be confidently ridden in adverse conditions.

YAMAHA TX750

A sophisticated roadster, with light sensitive steering, TX750 has a single overhead camshaft air cooled twin cylinder engine. The designers had considered using a four-cylinder unit but decided instead to develop a form of balancing unit which is claimed to give the twin the same smoothness as a four, without the associated size and complexity.

Relatively light for its size and power, Yamaha's biggest machine is as easy to handle as a middle size roadster. Apart from most attractive styling, features include five-way adjustable rear suspension, pressure fed dry sump lubrication and aluminium wheel rims.

Moto Guzzi V7 750.

63

This extraordinary motorcycle was built by the Wolseley car company in 1913 on behalf of a Russian Count who needed it to tour his estates. The huge

machine was held upright by a massive gyroscope, but proved difficult to ride.

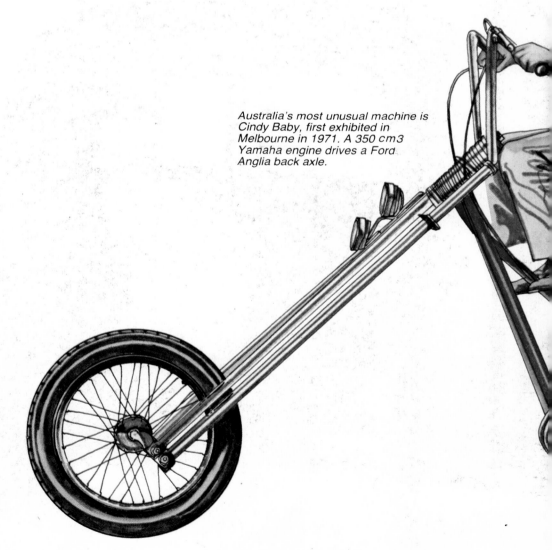

Australia's most unusual machine is Cindy Baby, first exhibited in Melbourne in 1971. A 350 cm3 Yamaha engine drives a Ford Anglia back axle.

Count Peter Schilowsky looked a typical European Count when he approached the Wolseley Car Company in 1913. His appearance created no surprise — but his request did. He asked the British company to build him the largest two-wheeler ever made.

Explaining that his Russian estates were interwoven by narrow, winding pathways, normally travelled on horse or by foot, he unfolded an armful of drawings which revealed his plan. It was a monster motorcycle which could stay upright, when stationary, by means of a large gyroscope. There was seating for four, a powerful four cylinder engine and a pair of small sprag wheels which, when lowered, supported the machine while the engine was not running.

The Count had worked out every detail. A gyroscope is virtually a large top that always stays upright when spinning rapidly, so he arranged for two pendulums to control it. Should the vehicle have leant to either side, the pendulums would bring the gyroscope into action, causing the vehicle to straighten up immediately.

The Wolseley people had some misgivings, but they agreed to build the unusual design. Eventually, a long narrow four seater motorcycle was produced. Though it exhibited some curious faults (such as leaning the wrong way on corners) the design was considered sufficiently workable to be handed over to the enterprising Count.

Unfortunately, he could not be found. His Russian estates had been over-run during the revolution then sweeping his country and he had fled. Until 1955 the large and ponderous machine was a prize exhibit in Wolseley's museum — a memento of the day when wealthy private men could afford to pioneer ideas that were ahead of their time. In 1955 it was taken apart and scrapped.

Almost 50 years later Ford Motor Company produced an updated version of the same idea — an experimental Gyron two-wheeler with gyroscopic stabilizer. Though it never went into production, the prototype provided some valuable engineering data.

The Russian-designed machine was the first of many oddball motorcycles, some built here, others overseas.

Perhaps the most unusual Australian design was Cindy Baby, a wild show machine exhibited first in 1971. Its appearance strongly suggested Cinderella and the fairy godmother who turned a pumpkin into a handsome coach. Far from being built by the touch of a wand, however, Cindy Baby was a professional engineering effort, with a 350 cc Yamaha motorcycle engine driving a Ford Anglia differential and back axle. A three wheeler chassis frame with chopper-style front forks and wide fat racing tyres provided the platform for the bright orange 'pumpkin'. A special seat for the coachman and lavish use of chrome plating added to the spectacular appearance. Plushly upholstered, the four-seat accommodation was the most comfortable to be found on any motorcycle in the world.

Cindy Baby could not be driven on public roads, but a large number of other custom-built motorcycles are used extensively on long road trips.

The art of customising was born in the USA before the second world war. Only recently has it become popular in Australia, and several firms have been established to cater exclusively for the growing demand. During 1973 'customising' of motorcycles became illegal in several States.

Highly customised cycles are often referred to as choppers, especially when the front forks are extended — Californian style — for greater rake (incline from the perpendicular). The name dates to the days when in the USA big Harley Davidson and Indian motorcycles were stolen, then 'chopped down' and changed so as not to be recognisable. Today the business is entirely legitimate and factory designs are modified to give the owner a more distinctive machine than can be bought off the showroom floor.

John Hadlow, manager of Australia's best known chopper firm before the new laws were introduced, says that the biggest job he had handled cost $1,400 above the price of the original motorcycle. The end result was a spectacular BSA, fitted with Norton engine, highly modified frame, Californian style front forks, custom paint job, plush seating, remodelled fuel tank, widened rear wheel and a smaller, narrow front wheel.

The art of successful customising is to give the owner exactly what he wants. His machine must stand out in a crowd, even a crowd of choppers. There are certain basic changes which follow established practice, or the work can be done to the exclusive

Extensive customising is no longer legal in some Australian States but some superb machines have been built and are still in use. Sydney specialist John Hadlow built this one.

order of the client. The fuel tank may be reworked with dished sides, or replaced by one of many stock designs whose name takes after the shape — Banana, Peanut, Coffin or Sportster.

Upholsterers create special saddles, sometimes known as 'trick' seats. The most popular of these is the King and Queen, in which the pillion passenger sits higher than the rider and looks over his shoulder. Choppers are often used for touring, so the seats are well padded for long distance comfort. One popular variation is to have a pair of fancy solo seats, one behind the other, each with a short back rest. Riders who prefer to travel alone often have a single high backed seat with decorative pleating.

Exhaust pipes, usually featured, can be made to any shape. Sissy bars — those tall back rests seen on many choppers — were born when some US States made it mandatory for a passenger grab rail to be fitted behind the pillion. The rails became increasingly featured on custom bikes, culminating in the elongated shapes seen today.

The most spectacular visual change is to extend the forks, bringing the front wheel ahead of its normal position. The effect is to enhance riding comfort and high speed road stability, with some loss of steering manoeuvrability in traffic.

To achieve Californian style forks, a customiser remodels the frame, giving extra rake to the steering neck. Usually the forks are extended by no more than 205 mm (8 ins), so that the original handling characteristics are not drastically changed. The new fork legs are fabricated from one piece of special high tensile steel for extra strength. Usually 'tweek bars' are fitted to brace the centre of the forks, reducing any tendency to twist. Tweek bars can also be moved in position to adjust the tension of the front suspension springs.

Custom handlebars can be made to almost any shape, with comfort and appearance the main considerations. The various styles are named after their shape, such as Z-bars, T-bars, Pull-backs and six bend Pull-backs.

Considerable chrome is used to decorate most choppers and the paint job is always something special. Automotive lacquers and acrylics are used, often with a metallic finish. As choppers are usually stripped of everything except the bare necessities, special attention becomes focused on the paintwork. So, if it is a work of art, so much the better. If this is not accomplished, the aim is to turn the paint into a theme of expression which is why, in the search for individuality, some machines become a maze of complex designs and details.

Specially useful in paint customising is an air brush. Used delicately, it permits intricate shading and the production of featured highlights such as imitation bullet holes, spatters or webbing. Loops and spaghetti edging, popular on contemporary designs are done by laying out a free pattern of thin masking tape. The area is then worked over with the air brush and the tape removed. Fish scales are done by pressing a thumb against the panel and outlining with the air brush. Flames, loops, lace, sunburst and rainbow overlaps are produced by combining airbrush shading with tape patterns.

Choppers are usually built by modifying a showroom bike but some enthusiasts prefer to leave the appearance unchanged and modify the power plant. One Sydney owner replaced the twin cylinder engine of his BMW with a four cylinder Volkswagen unit — a job more easily done that might be expected. Melbourne enthusiast, Roger Sonnenreim, also used a BMW as the basis for the world's first rotary motorcycle. In 1968 he installed a 10.5 hp Fitchel and Sachs Wankel engine which weighed only 13.6 kg (30 lbs) compared with 31.6 kg (70 lbs) for the original engine. Since then several leading motorcycle firms have developed experimental rotary motorcycles.

Perhaps the most ambitious engine transplant yet made was the handywork of 'Wild' Bill Belbe of Boscobel, USA. He built a $35,000 custom machine, powered by a Chevrolet engine, stopped by disc brakes, steered by hydraulic power and parked by jacks.

Another USA innovation was Monster Cycle, conceived and built by Jay Ohrberg of Hollywood, California.

'It'll go faster than anyone would dare to drive it, so we'll never know the top speed,'

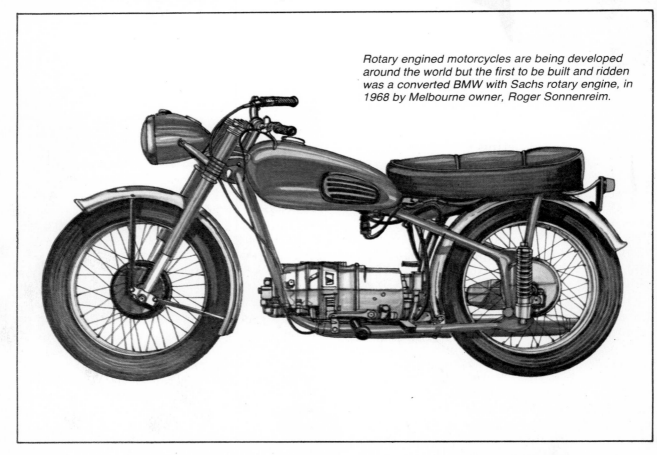

Rotary engined motorcycles are being developed around the world but the first to be built and ridden was a converted BMW with Sachs rotary engine, in 1968 by Melbourne owner, Roger Sonnenreim.

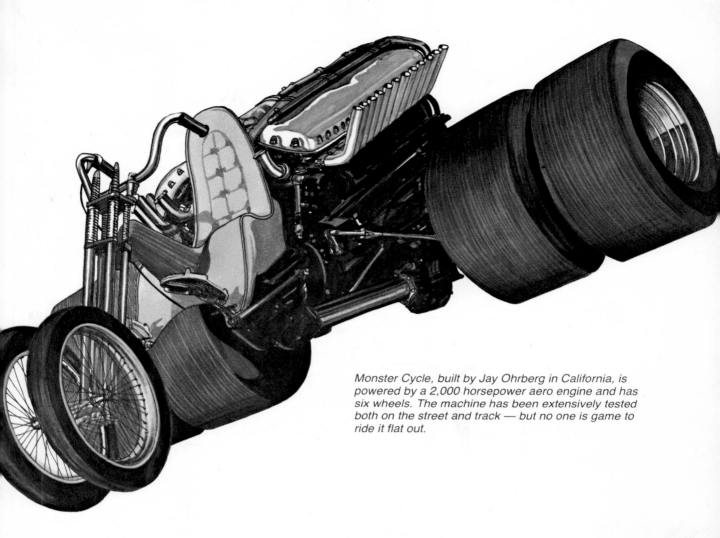

Monster Cycle, built by Jay Ohrberg in California, is powered by a 2,000 horsepower aero engine and has six wheels. The machine has been extensively tested both on the street and track — but no one is game to ride it flat out.

he said, after completing the monster. And indeed it would, as the huge machine was powered by a twelve cylinder 2000 hp aero engine.

Monster Cycle rests on a fork-type end, with dual front wheels to take the weight. The hand laced wheels are shod with Land Speed Record tyres. Despite its appearance, Monster Cycle is a truly functional machine that has been extensively driven on test runs. With a thirst that gobbles up fuel at the rate of 18 litres (four gallons) a minute, it may not be an ideal town bike, but at least there is no fear of finding one parked at the nearby supermarket.

Motorcycle manufacturers have become so versatile in their design techniques that there is less need now than ever to custom-build a freak design, unless you want to explore new ground.

For example, the early three-wheelers (trikes to the trade) were home made — they just could not be bought. Today, a variety of models is on the production line. The world's largest motorcycle maker — Honda — make two, both of which can be seen in Australia.

ATC is a relatively new designation, meaning all-terrain-cycle, Honda's pair being known as ATC 70 and ATC 90. Being the smaller and cheaper model, 70 is the more popular. It is virtually a mini exploration vehicle, at its best on mud, slush, snow marsh and grass. Its balloon-like tyres are vulnerable to sharp rocks, so it is best suited to soft conditions.

A squat little bike with jaunty appearance and fat do-nut tyres, it attracts attention wherever it goes. As the engine drives both back wheels, the machine needs a very special riding technique. For tight bends, it is best to lift the outer wheel and go around on two wheels, but for slippery conditions both rear wheels are needed for maximum stability and traction. Honda's ATC rides effortlessly over terrain where a two wheeled rider would normally vacate the saddle and push.

Another advantage is that the rider can trickle along at very slow speeds without putting down a foot to maintain balance. Water up to 255 mm (10 ins) deep can be crossed and it is little trouble to climb a grade as steep as 30 degrees.

Even the larger Honda 90 weighs under 91 kg (200 lbs) and can be readily dismantled, then carried in a car or waggon.

makers, accomplish this by means of a constant velocity ball joint at the top of the front forks. The joint is shaft driven from the gearbox, transmitting its power to the front sprocket by chains.

Trailbreaker is amazingly stable at low speeds and will trickle along at half walking pace without losing its balance. It also climbs the steepest and most slippery slopes imaginable.

Maximum speed is 49 kmh (30 mph), but Trailbreaker is happier cruising at 40 kmh (25 mph). For normal riding, the two gallon (9 litre) fuel tank gives around eight hours of bush bashing, but the big hollow wheels act as supplementary fuel tanks and can

A two-wheeled car? That's what Ford had in mind when they designed this gyroscopically controlled two-wheeler.

It will not go into production but it may well influence motorcycle design in the future.

Though primarily a recreational vehicle for exploring and seeking remote fishing spots, Honda has its serious uses and can best be described as a FUNctional three-wheeler.

For those who believe that two wheels are better than three even on slippery terrain, the American built Trailbreaker is the answer. It can beat some of the toughest terrain to be found anywhere in Australia. The writer was one of the first to put the unusual machine through its paces and quickly discovered that it is almost unstoppable.

The reason is that Trailbreaker is the world's first two-wheel-drive motorcycle. Power from a single cylinder engine is transmitted to both front and rear wheels by means of chains, giving twice the normal traction on slippery surfaces.

Simple though this idea seems, there is a major complication: the front wheel must be steered as well as powered. Rokon Inc, the

take a further 33 litres (7.5 gallons). The ground clearance is 480 mm (15 ins) and low pressure cleated tyres provide a freakish ability to penetrate the innermost secrets of the countryside.

Interesting technical features include an automatic torque converter and two wheel disc brakes. The overall weight is surprisingly light, 83 kg (185 lbs), and Trailbreaker proves a surprisingly easy machine to ride. The only controls are a hand accelerator, gear lever and handbrake. Even a luggage platform is standard!

A growing number of ATC trikes are coming here, mainly from the USA. Many have colourful lightweight fibreglass bodies and compact dimensions, allowing them to be carried in large cars or waggons.

One spectacular design is the US-built Tricart, which has already proved its toughness by winning long and difficult off-road races. Tricart has an aircraft type monocoque fibreglass shell in which the body, chassis, seats, engine compartment and gas tank are built into a single unit. It weighs less than 102 kg (225 lbs) and is not difficult to lift on to a vehicle for transportation.

There is limited seating room, so the passenger rides pick-a-back behind the rider.

Essentially a fun trike, it is at home on snow, sand, mud and grass and is amphibious enough to tackle deep water. One of its virtues is an ability to make incredibly tight bends in a perfectly controlled slide. Tricart can also climb steep slippery slopes and cruise at 72 kmh (45 mph) on smooth terrain. The 11 hp two-stroke engine has enough power to make an impressive wheel

The first two-wheeled-drive Trail Breaker to come to Australia was seen by millions of television viewers as a demonstration rider showed its astonishing ability to climb steep, muddy slopes. It is the only motorcycle in the world with drive to front and rear wheels.

Motorcycle components plus a three-wheeled concept give the US made Dunecycle the ability to tackle a wide variety of terrain, from soft marsh to hard snow.

stand when starting from rest.

Controls are anything but conventional. The steering system can be operated by hand or knee—or both; the brakes are applied by pushing the handlebars forward.

Tri-Sport is another US product seen here in small numbers. Sold with the slogan, 'Three-wheeling, free-wheeling', it comes in five models ranging from a 3 hp miniature for junior to a twenty horsepower machine weighing 113 kg (250 lbs). All models have fibreglass bodies, with overall lengths varying from 1500 to 2150 mm (59 to 81 ins). Steering is conventional with motorcycle type handlebars but an interesting feature is that the front wheel can be quickly replaced with a ski for use on snow.

Dunecycle, the smallest and cheapest of the US designs, is able to tackle almost any terrain including water up to 280 mm (12 ins) in depth. It weighs only 50 kg (110 lbs) and fits into the boot of a large car, the overall length being 1700 mm (68 ins), width 1160 mm (46 ins) and height 760 mm (31 ins).

Big flotation tyres make it a combined buggy and snowmobile and the gaily coloured fibreglass body can be seen from miles away. No gear shifting is necessary as the 5 hp engine drives a torque converter. One unusual control is the provision of separate brakes for the rear wheels. This allows the driver to reduce any tendency to wheel spin on slippery surfaces and to make tight turns by locking the inner wheel.

There are times when three wheels can be even more fun than two!

Is there a future for unusual designs? Yes! It is more than likely that two and three wheelers will be increasingly used for off-road recreational purposes. The scope for original ideas is enormous, as off-roading embraces anything from amphibious buggies to all-terrain-vehicles conquering mountain goat country.

Evel Knievel, the top U.S. motorcycle stunt man, has built a Skycycle with which he plans to jump Snake River Canyon in Idaho. The bike looks like a two-wheeled rocket and is equipped with wings and parachute. The plan is to roar up a 100 metre ramp, powered by solid propellent rockets, to a speed of 560 km/h (350 mph) and then soar into the sky. Hopefully the intrepid stunt man will cross the 1.2 km (¾ mile) canyon and land by parachute on the other side.

More down to earth machines than this are inevitable for mass production. Undoubtedly, the near future holds some exciting and novel designs.

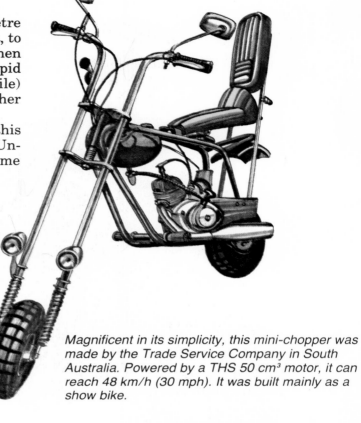

Magnificent in its simplicity, this mini-chopper was made by the Trade Service Company in South Australia. Powered by a THS 50 cm³ motor, it can reach 48 km/h (30 mph). It was built mainly as a show bike.

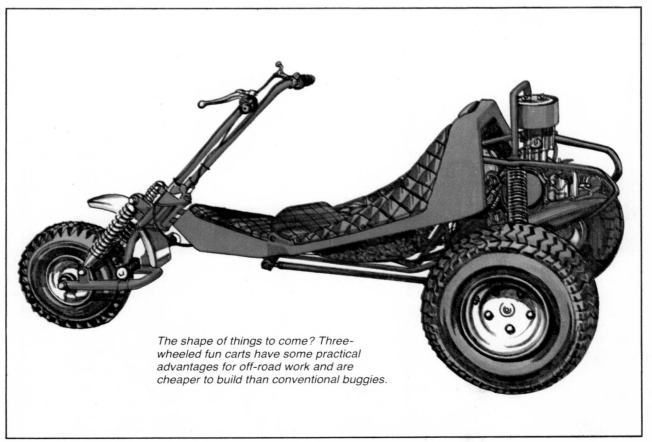

The shape of things to come? Three-wheeled fun carts have some practical advantages for off-road work and are cheaper to build than conventional buggies.

LOOKING BACK

Three thousand years ago an enterprising citizen of the Babylonian empire had a bright idea. He joined a pair of crude wooden wheels with a bar, sat on the bar and pushed his 'bicycle' along with his feet. As a conveyance it was hardly practical — but no doubt his friends and neighbours found it an amusing curiosity.

Strangely enough no one thought of fitting pedals to a similar machine until Kirkpatrick MacMillan of Scotland produced the first rideable bicycle as recently as 1839.

Heavy and cumbersome, it was at least a beginning. A few years later another inventor produced a lighter, more practical bicycle. This was dubbed the Penny-Farthing, after coins in use at the time, because the bicycle consisted of a large driving wheel at the front with a small stabilising wheel at the rear. The rider perched on a small saddle over the front wheel, operating pedals attached to the wheel hub.

The Penny-Farthing rapidly became a fashionable plaything as well as a convenient means of getting around on smooth level roads.

In 1885 the brilliant German engineer, Gottlieb Daimler, was looking for a way to test a new lightweight four-stroke engine he had designed. He had planned to build a four-wheeled carriage to be powered by the new engine but first he needed a simple machine as a test bed. He therefore built a bicycle, installed the ¾ hp engine and set off on a trouble-free trip of 29 km (18 miles).

That he was riding the world's first successful motorcycle was of little interest to Daimler. He was more concerned with the operation of the engine, which, he felt, would revolutionise transport.

By today's standards, the Daimler motorcycle was unbelievably crude, being built hurriedly by hand, at a time when there was nothing else to copy. No suspension system was fitted and as even the best roads were rough, to call it a bone-shaker is an understatement.

Nevertheless, the basic idea was sound and its appearance coincided with an equally brilliant development. John Boyd Dunlop, another Scotsman, had produced the first successful air-filled rubber tyres. They were intended to smooth the ride of a normal horse-drawn carriage but proved even more suitable for the higher speeds possible with a motorised vehicle.

The two inventions caught the imagination of enthusiasts around the world. An almost feverish race began to produce motorised vehicles in countries as far apart as Australia and France. Designs progressed so quickly that in 1903 the Dunlop Tyre company ran a magazine advertisement proudly proclaiming '18,000 miles (28,500 km) on a motorcycle fitted with Dunlop tyres'.

Early motorcycling was sometimes the subject of ridicule. In 1897, for example, the Horseless Vehicle Journal published a report of a race between a cycle and motorcycle. The two-man event lasted one hour, at the end of which the cyclist had covered 43 km (27 miles) and the motorcycle rider was 270 metres (300 yards) behind, his final lap being accompanied by the jeers of a crowd, jubilant that the motorcycle was beaten.

There is little reliable evidence about the earliest days of motorcycling in Australia.

Newspapers of the day did not consider the subject worthy of detailed comment, but one observer, Mr E. Lincoln, was probably close to the truth with a report in the 1905 edition of the NSW Motorists and Cyclists Annual.

He wrote:

'When motors and motor cars were nascent in Paris, Berlin and London, a man in Brisbane made an attempt to produce a motor that would drive a bicycle. This was in 1893. The man was Mr Knight Eaton, who was then manager in Brisbane for the Austral Cycle Agency. His motor, which was practically made by himself, was fitted to the back of a bicycle, right behind the rear wheel. The motor was not a success — it proving more a freak than anything else. This is the first recorded attempt in Australia to apply a motor to a bicycle or to travelling road machines of that class.'

The 1905 report went on as follows:—

'In the middle of 1898, Messrs Gavin Gibson Ltd, of Sydney, imported seven motor tricycles and it is said that these were the first motor machines ever brought into Australia. In 1895 the first motor tricycle was made in Sydney and various people tried without success to manufacture motorcycles. In 1898, for example, Messrs G. W. Wood, of Leichhardt, NSW, built a motor bicycle but it was not a complete success. In fact, it was not until 1901 that two motor cycles were imported into Australia from America. One was bought by Dr Farrell, of Quirindi, the other by Mr J. McKinney, of Nagus Station, Gundagai. These are believed to have been the first really workable motor cycles in the country.'

In later years many motorcycles were designed and built in Australia. For example, the Lewis was built in Adelaide from 1903 to 1905, many being sold, both air cooled and water cooled models. Another well-known South Australian design was the Favourite, of which nearly fifty were built during 1914 and 1915.

By that time motorcycles had become reliable, practical machines, suitable for long trips. But this was far from the case in earlier times. Riding during the pioneer years was an unpredictable adventure, because designers had not learned the art of making the machines handle or steer well. Tyres were skinny and likely to go into a slide on corners. Engines were cantankerous, often inexplicably refusing to start, perhaps for days on end. Punctures were a dime a dozen.

But right from the start men and women recognised the immense potential of the motorcycle both for pleasure riding and as everyday transport.

Design improvements came thick and fast, culminating in the enormous range of different makes and models now sold. An estimated 40 million motorcycles are in use around the world, with 4 million new machines built each year, Japan being the leading producer.

Australia's motorcycle population is about 250,000, with new annual sales in the vicinity of 73,000 machines. Only a few specialised sporting designs are built here, the vast majority of cycles being imported. The reason is that overseas manufacturing costs are far lower than would be possible in Australia because automated mass production techniques are economically possible only when building for world markets.

WHERE TO SEE HISTORIC MOTORCYCLES

Many museums around Australia have displays of motorcycles. The largest collection is at Birdwood Mill Motor Museum,

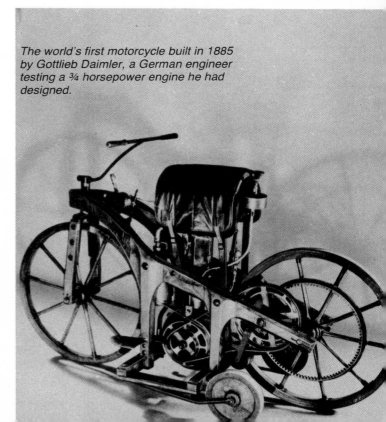

The world's first motorcycle built in 1885 by Gottlieb Daimler, a German engineer testing a ¾ horsepower engine he had designed.

located at Birdwood, just 28 miles from Adelaide, South Australia. Seventy five historic motorcycles and 25 equally interesting old cars are housed in one of the most up-to-date museum buildings in the world. Visitors can see some vehicles in action on a special demonstration circuit and there is a huge range of other exhibits (including aircraft and marine) in a historic and tranquil setting, which includes the original steam powered Randall Mill. The motorcycle display has several machines designed and built in Australia.

Many of the historic photographs in these pages are reproduced by courtesy of Mr Gavin Sandford-Morgan, chairman of Birdwood museum.

Gilltraps Gold Coast Museum, who also provided photographic assistance, is located at Coolangatta, Queensland. In addition to a display of 68 historic cars, the museum has 11 motorcycles and a rare collection of very old bicycles. A feature of the museum is that there are daily demonstrations of many exhibits.

Fifteen years separate this 1886 Humber Tandem tricycle and one of the first powered cycles — a 1901 Singer with 258 cm³ single cylinder rear engine.
Top to bottom: A 1904 Minerva, 1925 Rudge, 1929 Harley Davidson Super Pup, 1926 Norton with sidecar, a race winning 1948 'Manx' Norton.